Black Americans
In The 21st Century

INTEGRATING OR SEGREGATING

Doug Saint Carter

HEYDAY
PUBLISHING, Inc.

2013

Table of Contents

Chapter 1
WE STILL ANGRY

The question is not only why are black African Americans so racially angry, but - toward whom is all this anger directed?

Several months ago during Black History month I caught a TV special, "Way Black When," hosted by comedian Sinbad on the black cable channel TV One. The program was designed to reflect back on the golden age of black culture that emerged during the 1970s, '80s, and '90s. Many of the guests were eager to discuss experiences of racial discrimination, a favorite topic of the host. But Jayne Kennedy, the first African American woman to win Miss Ohio USA in 1970, the first woman to join the staff of CBS Sports' "NFL Today," and a successful actor, gave no indication of racial animosity. Yet Sinbad was determined to pry out of her any kind of acknowledgement that she had experienced anything that could be defined as racial mistreatment. When she gave in to his manipulation, Sinbad took the opportunity to turn to the camera and say, "we still angry." Poor grammar aside, we're left to wonder how long this ongoing, never-ending grudge culture towards whites will continue. It's already lasted for hundreds of years and no matter how much things have improved for blacks, like a deadly plague, it devastates the living. Integrating or segregating? Both, apparently. It's whichever one is thought to be the most convenient or beneficial at a given time.

Is there any question which one Rev. Al Sharpton was thinking August 28, 2011 at a dedication ceremony for the Dr. Martin Luther King Jr. monument, when he said, "Get ready, George Washington. There's a new neighbor on the Potomac. Get ready, Mr. Jefferson. There's a new neighbor on the Potomac. Get ready Mr. Lincoln. There's a new neighbor, and were all (blacks) coming to help him move in. We brought our luggage. We brought our food. Guess who's coming to dinner?" Too bad Sharpton's luggage is filled with hate and grudges, and that food he brought is the epitome of bitterness. Where is love?

During a time when Americans have our first black president, Barack Obama, whom many of us hoped would be the great racial unifier, Sharpton goes with his usual divisive lack of class. Why is it that all of America's black leaders, black spokespeople and black organizations continue to be living roadblocks to racial harmony? A wise white man wanted me to remind Al Sharpton, the slaves didn't free themselves.

Speaking of President Barack Obama, almost immediately after he was elected into office, a national poll was taken to sample how many people thought electing a black president would improve race relations.

At that time, 76% thought it would, 10% thought it would not. Unhappily I fell into the 10% category. The reason being, I knew it would give so much more exposure to the racially divisive attitude of blacks than most non-blacks were aware of. Of course, as that 76% began to slide and the 10% rise, the media focused mainly on white folks as racist. The fact is whites have matured racially a great deal over the past several decades, while blacks in general choose to maintain a divisive attitude, marinated in anger.

There are white hate groups which the general white population wants no part of, while the general black African American population is in lockstep with all the negative skin color mania. Thank goodness there is a small percentage of black African Americans who don't believe in and want no part of all the racial negativity.

It cannot be denied that Louis Farrakhan and the New Black Panther Party are well known American elements of hate within the black population. One of their main goals is to keep blacks racially angry and divisive. So far, mission accomplished. That should be a wake-up call for all.

It's ironic that the American black population is so racially competitive with the white population. The white population is essentially unaware of this competition and is not involved in competing. Blacks are losing a competition with someone who's not competing with them. If it weren't so tragic it would be hilarious. Blacks must be doing something wrong. Could it be their lopsided political affiliation or simply that being racially divisive lacks fairness, understanding, and most importantly, common sense?

When it comes to race relations, the 'N' word we should be most concerned with these days is negativity.

This book, *Black Americans In The 21ˢᵗ Century*, is a re-release of the book, *Drinking From the Cup: One Man's Experiences, Efforts and Observations of Improving Race Relations*, which I published in 2008. The only difference is the title, which should bring more attention to the topic, and this additional chapter, "We Still Angry." The first book did very poorly in sales which I believe, in large part, was due to the title, which came from a line in a Dr. Martin Luther King Jr. speech: "Learn to love your white brothers and sisters, don't drink from the cup of bitterness, hate and grudges" – A line I have never heard another living individual speak, other than myself.

It may take generations before my target audience, black African Americans, discover this book. I believe it's because they have no interest in improving race relations or taking any responsibility for the endless divisive stalemate. Hopefully blacks in the future will come to realize how detrimental their racial attitude has been, not only to themselves, but all Americans in general.

Certainly there has been enough racial negativity since 2008 to write an entire new book. However, my purpose of involvement is to improve race relations. Although there have been many new incidents, the racial attitude thoroughly covered in my first book still prevails.

I do feel the need to update a couple of things that are not in book No. 1. What's most astonishing to me is how blacks have come up with a new form of racism to complain about, which I missed the first time. That is, "Structural Racism." As it's defined, it sounds like something Louis Farrakhan or the New Black Panther Party or someone with their hideous and evil mindset came up with. It's too ridiculous to waste the ink or paper to print here.

Another thing that begs coverage is a June 2011 article by an African American professor of economics at George Mason University, "Black Silence on Black Racism is 'Betrayal'" by Walter E. Williams.

In part the article states that today most racist assaults are committed by blacks. What's worse is that there are blacks, still alive, who lived through the times of lynching, Jim Crow and open racism who remain silent in the face of it.

WE STILL ANGRY

Last year, four black Skidmore College students yelled racial slurs while they beat up a white man because he was dining with a black man. Skidmore College's first response was to offer counseling to one of the black students charged with the crime. In 2009, a black Columbia University professor assaulted a white woman during a heated argument about race relations. According to interviews and court records obtained and reported by Denver's ABC affiliate (Dec.4, 2009), black gangs roamed downtown Denver, verbally venting their hatred for white victims before assaulting and robbing them during a four-month crime wave. Earlier this year, two black girls beat a white girl at a McDonald's, and the victim suffered a seizure. Chicago Mayor Rahm Emanuel ordered an emergency shutdown of the beaches in Chicago because mobs of blacks were terrorizing families. According to the NBC affiliate (June 8), a gang of black teens stormed a city bus, attacked white victims and ran off with their belongings.

Racist black attacks are against not only whites but also Asians. In San Francisco, five blacks beat an 83-year-old Chinese man to death. They threw a 57-year-old woman off a train platform. Two black Oakland teenagers assaulted a 59-year-old Chinese man. The punching knocked him to the ground, killing him. At Philly's South Philadelphia High School, Asian students report that black students routinely pelt them with food and beat, punch and kick them in school hallways and bathrooms as they hurl epithets such as "Hey, Chinese!" and "Yo, Dragon Ball!" The Asian American Legal Defense and Education Fund charged the School District of Philadelphia with "deliberate indifference" toward black victimization of Asian students.

In reporting of many of the brutal attacks, the news media make no mention of the race of the perpetrators. If it were white racist gangs randomly attacking blacks, the mainstream media would have no hesitation reporting the race of the perps. Editors for the *Los Angeles Times*, *The New York Times* and *Chicago Tribune* admitted to deliberately censoring information about black crime for political reasons. *Chicago Tribune* Editor Gerould Kern recently said that the paper's reason for censorship was to "guard against subjecting an entire group of people to suspicion."

These racist attacks can, at least in part, be attributed to the black elite, who have a vested interest in racial paranoia. And that includes a president (Barack Obama) who has spent years aligned with people who have promoted racial grievance and polarization, and who appointed an Attorney General (Eric Holder) who's accused us of being "a nation of cowards" on matters of race and has refused to prosecute black thugs who gathered at a Philadelphia voting site in blatant violation of federal voter intimidation laws. Tragically, black youngsters, seething with resentments, refusing to accept educational and other opportunities unknown to blacks yesteryear, will turn out to be the larger victims in the long run.

Black silence in the face of black racism has to be one of the biggest betrayals of the civil rights movement that included black and white Americans.

One thing about that article that needs to be stressed is the harm done to black youth by parenting and grandparenting. As long as grandparents and parents teach their grandchildren and children not to like whites, not to trust whites, not to act like whites etc., we all lose.

I'm always hearing blacks say, "we've come a long way, but we have a long way to go." If blacks continue their negative racial attitude, that "long way to go" will be a journey with no end.

On a personal note from that article, I hope Attorney General Eric Holder reads this book, so he'll know we're not all cowards on matters of race. Come to think of it, he's probably too cowardly to take on this book.

In the chapters to come, you'll learn I took part in a months-long study to improve black and white race relations in Jacksonville, Florida which got underway in 2001. During that time I made the point that the very fact we are having such a study meant we have formed a ball, but the ball is not rolling. At this writing in late 2012 (and I'm sure for years to come) it's still up to blacks to put that ball in play, as it sits motionless for the world to see. Where is love?

Chapters two through fourteen were originally the book, *Drinking From The Cup*, which one reviewer from South Florida described as "informative, insightful and inflammatory." No matter how harsh the contents may appear I still regard everyone as an individual and any prejudice I may have is purely personal. Many blacks accuse me of lumping them all together. That's crazy. Blacks are the only population I'm aware of that constantly refer to themselves as "us," "we," "my people," "our people," "our community", "our neighborhoods" and so on. Who's lumping who? As with whites, blacks and all other non-blacks, I love some of them and don't care so much for some of them, as I try to exercise fairness, understanding and common sense. God (or whomever or whatever is preferred) bless.

Print publication was temporarily delayed so the following could be included;

Drinking From the Cup was published the week of the 2008 presidential election, leaving me unaware of who won before the book was published. This time I know President Barack Obama won a second term.

I plan to send the president and first lady a copy of *Black Americans in the 21st Century*, with a copy of the letter which follows.

When I wrote the letter, a strong sense of optimism came over me: What if the president contacts me and shows a sincere interest in reaching out to help? How unbelievably wonderful that would be!

Not long after, a stronger sense of reality set in, reminding me of how disappointing my experiences, efforts, and observations of improving race relations have been.

President Barack Obama is multiracial but considers himself black. At least it's my understanding that on the last census form, under the category of race, he checked "black," not "white" or "other."

With all respect to our president and the office of the president, I am deeply aware there is no known individual that is a black African American who shows the slightest interest in putting forth an effort to improve black and white race relations. So, why would the leader of the free world, who is black, opt to improve humanity over jeopardizing the black Democratic voting block? Sadly, America, the great racial unifier has yet to be found. Where is love?

November 7, 2012

Barack Obama
The President
The White House
1600 Pennsylvania Avenue, N.W.
Washington, DC 20500

Dear Mr. President,

Congratulations on your second-term victory.

With the understanding that you enjoy reading, I hope you'll consider reading my newest book (included with this letter), *Black Americans in the 21st Century: Integrating or Segregating.*

You once said, "If you want to make a difference in race relations, you have to join the fray." That's something I did many years ago, and I need as much help now as I did then just to be heard.

No doubt you won't agree with every point I make from cover to cover. I regret some of them. However it will be a severe disappointment if you disagree with the purpose of my book, which is to establish not only the need to improve race relations, but to focus on where the greatest amount of responsibility lies in present-day America.

Mr. President, humanity is calling. Please answer. Together we can make sure your legacy includes being historically remembered as America's first great racial unifier.

Most respectfully,

Doug Saint Carter
Heyday Publishing Inc.
P.O. Box 8925
Jacksonville, FL
32239

Cc: First Lady Michelle Obama

Chapter 2
DRINKING FROM THE CUP

Dr. Martin Luther King Jr. said in one of his many acclaimed speeches, "Learn to love your white brothers and sisters; don't drink from the cup of bitterness and hate." My sole purpose for writing this book is to contribute in some way to improving race relations between black and white Americans. Unfortunately, in these times, it is an unpopular task to undertake, and I anticipate some backlash. No doubt I'll receive a verbal black attack and, on occasion, displease some Caucasians. Where is Jesse Jackson when you really need him (for no other reason than his ability to rhyme)?

If I could give credit to two people for my interest in improving race relations, the first would be my father, and the second would be rhythm and blues/pop music pioneer, Jackie Wilson. While I was growing up, my father taught us that love has nothing to do with the color of your skin, and that we are all the same on the inside. My dad, at my request, took me to see Jackie Wilson a number of times in the early and mid-60s.

DRINKING FROM THE CUP

My first time seeing Jackie was in 1963—the same year that our city, Jacksonville, Florida, experienced some of the worst race riots it has ever seen. At all of the Jackie Wilson concerts we went to over the years, my father and I were among just a few dozen whites in a crowd of a few thousand blacks, but were never once made to feel unwanted or uncomfortable. I also give credit to Jackie Wilson himself, one of the early crossover artists, not because he was involved in race relations so much, but because of a book I wrote about him, and the experiences I had after it was published. Although Jackie would, on occasion, refuse to perform until the blacks in his audiences were allowed the same seating opportunity as whites, he rarely, if ever, spoke publicly about race. It should be noted, however, that because of his dynamic stage performance and ability to drive crowds into a frenzy, riots sometimes broke out. He was known as "Mr. Excitement." Many blacks eventually turned their backs on Jackie, in part because of his close ties with whites, and because primarily white backup singers were used on many of his hit recordings. This was an innovative strategy used by Jackie's record company to attract the white middle-class audience. I don't recall white audiences complaining that Elvis employed the Sweet Inspirations, who were black backup singers.

The title of my book, *The Black Elvis—Jackie Wilson*, was all it took to prove what I had already been aware of for most of my life; that a very large portion of the American black population jumps at any mention of race and turns it into something negative. Some whites didn't like the book title either, but for different reasons and to a much lesser extent. If you know the Jackie Wilson story, then you know that he was the Black Elvis Presley. Elvis even called himself the White Jackie Wilson. I have heard many blacks say that Elvis stole from Jackie. If they were being the least bit fair, they would use the term influenced rather than stole, and what artist *isn't* influenced by someone else?

One African-American fellow, who runs a popular Internet Web site devoted to artists of black (soul) music, e-mailed me after the book came out, saying that all Jackie Wilson fans, and all blacks, should be offended by the book's title. He went on to tell me that Jackie was a superstar when Elvis was still carrying peanut butter and banana sandwiches to school that his mama made for him. And, of course, that Elvis stole from Jackie. Another man, a black writer in San Francisco, interviewed me about the book. His thoughts were that my book title represented just another case of a black man needing validation from whites to receive the recognition he deserved. But Jackie himself was the catalyst for that moniker! According to reliable witnesses at the artists' first meeting in 1966, Jackie said, "They call me the Black Elvis Presley."

That's just a couple of many similar responses to the title of the book. Neither could be more inaccurate. Responding to the Web site owner, I said it sounded like he was full of racial hatred, and was probably more a part of America's racial problems than a solution. He wrote back, saying that he never claimed to be part of the solution, which could lead one to believe that he was proud of being part of the problem.

The fact that the Web site owner had incorrect information about Jackie Wilson didn't help. He was wrong to say that Elvis stole from Jackie. By the time Elvis Presley knew Jackie Wilson existed in 1956, he had already starred in the movie *Love Me Tender* and had a number of Billboard top-10 hits. At that time, Jackie was the unbilled lead singer of the group "Billy Ward and the Dominoes," and still known by his nickname "Sonny." Furthermore, Jackie, or "Sonny," was already performing three of Elvis' songs in his live Las Vegas performances, including "Don't Be Cruel," and Elvis was reportedly crazy about Jackie's rendition of the song. So the soul man from the Web site, like many other blacks I've spoken with, is either ignoring or rewriting history to make Elvis look like a thief. There is no question that Elvis became an instant fan of Jackie and started using some of what he saw and heard in his own performances. You can call it a two-way street.

Here's what Jackie had to say about it, "A lot of people have accused Elvis of stealing the black man's music when in fact, almost every black solo entertainer copied his stage mannerisms from Elvis." Jackie Wilson's very first hit as a solo artist in 1957, 'Reet Petite,' was called an Elvis knockoff by critics of the day. So clearly, Jackie was influenced by Elvis before Elvis was influenced by Jackie. I was particularly offended by these criticisms of my book's title because of my appreciation for Jackie as an artist. Anyone who actually read the book would have understood that I was not belittling his accomplishments—in fact, quite the opposite. It was this response to my book, which I saw as irrationally racial and negative, that further inspired me to get involved in improving black and white race relations in America.

One of the most ridiculous comments I heard about Jackie Wilson and race relations came from a black man who said that because he was black, Jackie's record company wouldn't put his picture on his album covers. This is another example of someone ignoring the facts to support negative notions. During his career with Brunswick records, from 1957 to 1975, 32 albums were released, and Jackie's photo was on all but three. This makes me think their decision about the covers had nothing to do with Jackie's race. The observations made by the writer from San Francisco about my choice of book title, indicating that it was an example of a black man needing validation from a white man for his accomplishments, are also way off base. To this day Elvis is known worldwide, while his black counterpart has slipped through the cracks and gone forgotten. While Jackie doesn't need praise from whites in particular, his wonderful legacy *is* underappreciated, and that is what I wanted to change by writing about it.

Anyone who really knows the story knows that Jackie called himself the Black Elvis, and Elvis consequently referred to himself as the white Jackie Wilson. They were good friends who loved, honored, and respected one another. Trading names was a sign of respect and admiration between them. They responded to the effects of being racial crossover artists with honor. My decision to entitle the book, *The Black Elvis-Jackie Wilson*, was an attempt to use the name of Elvis, the "Artist of the 20th Century," to bring much needed attention to Jackie, the man who was probably the best singer and performer the pop music world has ever known. Elvis is quoted as saying, "Jackie, with all you have going for you, you should be the biggest singer in the world."

Since both of these entertainers have been gone for many years, I couldn't understand why it was important for so many individuals to be bitter about the matter. I believe it was no coincidence that the only black radio station in Jacksonville, Florida, WSOL V101.5, playing Jackie Wilson's music at that time, stopped when my book was published. Could it be race played a part in that decision? Traditional white oldies stations in Jacksonville and surrounding communities continued to include selections of Jackie's music and contacted me for interviews.

I contacted the program director at WSOL to ask if he would like to give away several copies of my book to his listeners in exchange for mentioning where it could be purchased, a common practice in the broadcast industry. He asked me to send him a copy, which I did, and I never heard from him again. I left messages by voice mail, fax, e-mail, and even asked the station's receptionist to handwrite a message to the program director to be sure he was contacted. To this day, the radio station plays music by artists from that era, but not Jackie Wilson. Considering Jackie's incredible and versatile body of work, it leads me to believe that the black radio station dropped Jackie Wilson from its playlist either because I'm white or because the book title offended them or both.

My father, my other great example of positive race relations, expressed concern that the title, *The Black Elvis-Jackie Wilson*, would be troublesome and controversial. He suggested the title, *White King, Black King*. I thought that was pretty good, but I was determined to stick with my original title specifically because the relationship between Jackie and Elvis is an historic fact that rarely gets mentioned because of racial prejudices on the part of both blacks and whites.

The original title of my book was *My Heart Is Crying*, which comes from the lyrics of Jackie Wilson's signature song, "Lonely Teardrops," which he was singing when he collapsed on stage at the Latin Casino in Cherry Hill, New Jersey, on September 29, 1975. That was the original title that came to mind in 1984 after Jackie's death, but I had the nagging thought that it was too depressing for such a dynamic performer. I considered using the title *Mr. Excitement*, but Rhino Records released a Jackie Wilson box set that included a small pamphlet titled "Mr. Excitement," and I was concerned about copyright infringement.

After becoming directly involved in various efforts to improve race relations between blacks and whites, which will be the subject of upcoming chapters, it became clear to me that my father's suggestion of *White King, Black King* would have offended many blacks just the same as the title I chose. It has become increasingly clear to me that blacks find ways to feel offended by anything that has to do with whites. A large segment of the African-American population, and probably even some whites, will find reason to be offended by something on every page of this book, including the blank ones, because they allow themselves to be dominated by bitterness, hate, and grudges. For that reason, this book will not be the length of a novel like Tolstoy's *War and Peace*. I don't claim to cover all bases here, but I am attempting to be as objective as my observations allow. This book is about my own personal experience with attempts to improve race relations. We all know there are two sides to every story. Nowhere is that more evident than present-day race relations between blacks and whites. Times change rapidly in America, but many of us prefer to judge one another as though nothing has changed in hundreds of years. A quote from Oscar Wilde is fitting when it comes to discussing race relations for many Americans, "Most people are other people. Their thoughts are someone else's opinions, their lives a mimicry, their passions a quotation." Many factors contribute to this way of thinking, not the least of which is the advent of so many special interest groups, who seem to have a one-way street mentality.

Chapter 3
BEYOND THE TALK:
IMPROVING RACE RELATIONS
IN NORTHEAST FLORIDA

In the midst of defending the title of my book, I ran across a notice in the *Florida Times-Union* in September of 2001 about a public workshop called "Improving Race Relations: Beyond the Talk in Northeast Florida." The main focus of the study was mostly on the black and white population and was sponsored by the "Jacksonville Community Council, Inc." (JCCI)—I couldn't wait to sign up. The workshop was scheduled to last six months, but ended up being extended to nine. As it turned out, I was the only individual out of the initial 150 or so who attended every last one of the meetings. I was so dedicated because I didn't want to miss it if any black individuals came forward to encourage blacks to improve race relations with whites. I was hoping someone might suggest taking more responsibility for one's own station in life, or mention something about stopping the endless efforts of trying to make whites feel guilty about slavery, or anything else that might point us in the direction of racial harmony. Unfortunately, none of that ever happened. I have, to this day, never heard one living black person, locally or nationally, be that encouraging. Only the late Dr. Martin Luther King Jr. has been so magnanimous.

The JCCI study group was attended by mostly blacks and whites, with a few Asians and Hispanics in attendance. At the beginning of the study, the number of blacks and whites in attendance was fairly even, but as time progressed I saw a smaller percentage of blacks represented. The average age seemed to be 35 years and older. The attendants were referred to as committee members, consisting mostly of the general public coming from various professions in the local community, including educators, attorneys, council members, members of the clergy, and others. There was a three-member panel overseeing the proceedings, which included an African-American judge, Brian J. Davis, co-chair; a Caucasian political consultant, Bruce Barcelo, co-chair; and Ben Warner, another white man, who was at that time senior community planner of JCCI. His main responsibility was taking notes of each meeting.

Throughout the course of the 33 meetings, which spanned a nine-month period, I could only come to a few conclusions as to why blacks attended. It was either to complain about racial disparities that, in most cases, occurred decades or even centuries ago (many of the present-day complaints are about more of a class disparity than race). The other reason was to see what might be in it for them. For the record, there were 26 findings of matters concerning some blacks and some non-blacks that could be improved, and to date most of these have been successfully addressed. Anything that improves the quality of life for some Americans, improves America. I have mixed feelings about the JCCI study, but so far as reaching its stated goal of improving race relations between blacks and whites, I see no improvement at all. It is obvious to me that there will never be improvement until members of the American black population put forth a much more diligent effort in that direction.

Throughout the course of the study, committee members were asked to come to the microphone to make comments or ask questions. I did so on several occasions. Once I commented that the fact that we were gathered there to discuss race relations meant that we had formed a ball, but that currently the ball wasn't rolling (and it still isn't). It was sad to observe, but the black folks in attendance seemed as though they were interested in making white people feel guilty for things they aren't responsible for and for holding white people's feet to the flame in the name of slavery, and treating slavery as though it were a current event.

On the subject of slavery, I was recently in a Barnes & Noble bookstore and was disappointed to see so many books in the African-American section with slavery in the title. Some of those titles included, *Black Slave Owners*, *Remembering Slavery*; *The Willie Lynch Letter and the Making of Slaves*; *Up From Slavery*; *Slave Testimony*; *Life of a Slave Girl*; *The Sounds of Slavery*; *Celia, a Slave*; *Voices From Slavery*; *An Eyewitness History of Slavery in America*; *Twelve Years a Slave*; *Slave Nation*; *Narrative of the Life of Frederick Douglass, an American Slave*; and many of the other titles were very racially derogatory.

At one of the JCCI meetings, I approached the microphone to ask, "With all respect, is it possible that blacks are leaning on history as a guiding light to the future?" Panel member Judge Brian J. Davis replied, "We'll discuss that matter later privately." This never happened. The judge and I had previously lunched together, and I have a great deal of respect for him. But in my experience, black people prefer to move a conversation toward what they deem to be racial injustices, rather than accept responsibility for problems they are creating and exacerbating, many of which are not racism, but matters of class.

Throughout the course of the study, there was very little that both blacks and whites agreed upon. The vast majority of both races agreed about interracial marriages and relationships. They weren't in favor of it. Although there was some disagreement about that, there were a couple of individuals who were part of an organization, whose name I cannot recall, that supports interracial relationships. Their comments for the most part were passed over, and never really addressed.

I found it a little disturbing that on a few occasions, blacks would stand up and say, "Just because I'm pro-black doesn't mean I'm anti-white." It seems implausible that you could be pro- anything and not be against its opposite to some degree. Some of the well-meaning whites in attendance seemed to be overly sensitive, in a supportive way, to what some of the blacks were saying. It is my belief that this attitude does more harm than good. These overly sympathetic whites seemed to be buying into whatever the blacks were saying and not holding them responsible for improving race relations. The African-American population dictates the tone of race relations in America, and that tone is very negative. It seems the better off blacks become, the worse the attitude seems to get.

I believe that blacks have convinced themselves that anger, bitterness, hate, and grudges are the best roads to travel. There are whites who have a similar degree of negativity toward blacks. However, the majority of the white population does not feel that way. In my experience, I have yet to find one black individual, locally or nationally, with a voice within the American population who encourages blacks to get along with whites. For as much deserved praise as Dr. Martin Luther King Jr. receives from the black population, it seems that no one has followed his teachings in that respect. If there is someone doing so, the media seems to have absolutely no interest in letting us hear from them, although I seriously doubt such an individual exists.

Near the end of the JCCI study, we proceeded to the findings, conclusions, and recommendations. I came forward, both on the microphone and in print, requesting someone from the African-American population in attendance to contribute in a positive way to the efforts of improving black and white race relations. All I was talking about was some kind of attitude adjustment. I wasn't asking blacks to contribute anything of material value; no one was asking them to reach for their wallets or dip into their bank accounts. I was just challenging them to live up to King's request, "Learn to love your white brothers and sisters; don't drink from the cup of bitterness and hate."

At each of the meetings, three guests were invited to speak to the committee, followed by a segment of questions and comments. At one meeting, all of the guests were African-Americans speaking on various issues of race. They were Edward Hayes of Diversity Training Associates, Gwen Marlow from the Marlow Resource Group, and Charlene Taylor Hill of the Jacksonville Human Rights Commission. As usual, I could glean nothing from their talks that had anything to do with improving race relations.

Improving race relations only requires an adjustment in attitudes, becoming a *color-kind* society, encouraging racial harmony, accepting one another as individuals instead of treating them as representatives of an entire race. Specifically for blacks, this requires that they stop using economics as a reason for not getting along with whites. The current attitude sorely lacks fairness, understanding, or common sense. Racial payback at this point in time is taking the path of a loser. Blacks and whites alike could stand to lighten up a little. Where is the love?

When my turn came around during the Q & A period, I asked the panel, "Do blacks really even want to get along with whites? If so, where's the proof? If not, why not?" After a slight pause, Ms. Hill came forward and said that when blacks get together, the conversation usually comes around to slavery, and things spiral down from that point. Since my question was a yes or no question, I had no choice except to believe that her answer was no.

Shortly thereafter, Edward Hayes stood up, pointed at me, and said, "I'm going to take you to lunch," generating much applause, "...I'm buying!" which got more rousing applause from the attendees as he walked over to where I was seated and shook my hand. I never saw or heard from Mr. Hayes again. I would have loved to spend some time with him to better understand his views on diversity. I tried to contact him through JCCI's Ben Warner with no success. I was disappointed that he used me to make himself look good in the meeting, and then dropped the ball. I was genuinely interested in having a dialogue with him, but apparently he was not. This was just one more confirmation that the ball is not rolling. Whites can push on the ball all they want, but until blacks participate, nothing constructive is going to happen.

With one hand stretched out, palm up, blacks are saying, "Give us." They're asking that society give them affirmative action, give them money, give them 40 acres and a mule, give them their own state, give blacks a free college education, give quota hiring preferences, give leniency to their criminal element, and give reparations. The other hand is clenched in a fist, indicating, "We don't like you." Naturally this is an attitude completely devoid of fairness, understanding, or common sense. Anyone ever heard of the phrase "You can catch a lot more flies with honey than vinegar"? The blacks I'm speaking of seem to have an endless supply of vinegar.

At another of our weekly meetings about seven members of the North Florida clergy of various denominations were the speakers. Each spoke for several minutes on their efforts to encourage diversity and inclusion in their congregation. When it came time for the question and comment portion of the meeting, instead of asking committee members to go to the microphone, which was done at every other meeting, we were asked to write down our questions and then turn them in. The moderator would then read the questions to the clergy members for their response. As time to conclude the meeting neared, I feared my question wouldn't make the cut from the dozens that were submitted. All of a sudden there it was. My question went something like this: "Would it be possible to create a policy where each week, every church in Jacksonville would take a minute to encourage their congregation to improve race relations?"

Once the question was read, there was complete silence for a few moments. Finally, a clergy member from one of our larger churches, a white man, paused and said, "No, because a minute is not long enough." That answer got a few chuckles and a few dropped jaws, which seemed bizarre to me. I felt that we had an opportunity to not only make a change, but even to make history. And it was brushed off with a weak attempt at humor. The clergy members had been talking about inclusion and diversity but literally scoffed at a practical and simple idea to make a difference.

At a subsequent meeting, one of our speakers was then Mayor John Delaney, who said that in all the racial discrimination complaints that came to his office, 50 percent were not due to race at all—although he didn't give a breakdown as to which races were complaining or to the nature of their complaints. At the conclusion of that meeting, several people approached the mayor for glad-handing and the like. I was able to get his attention for just a few seconds and took that opportunity to tell him about the clergies' response to my suggestion. I was stunned by his response. He agreed with the clergies' answer by saying he "didn't like being preached to." At that point, someone else came up and got his attention. All I could think was that when you go to church you get preached to, and if encouraging racial harmony bothers anyone, then they're probably part of the problem, which I don't think Mayor Delaney was. He seemed to have a lot of support from blacks and whites on racial issues, but his answer puzzles me to this day.

There were many examples of alleged racial discrimination brought out during the course of this study. One that nobody seemed to disagree with was the high rate of prison or jail time given to blacks in relation to all other races. Though the statistics prove this to be a fact, no one seems willing to give the criminal justice system any understanding with the problems they face. One of our guests from the Sheriff's Department said the police go to where they're called, and if that happens to be a highly black populated area, that's where they're going. Doesn't that make common sense?

If the police, attorneys, judges, and everyone involved in the criminal justice system consistently see not only a higher rate of crimes committed by blacks, but also a higher rate of black return offenders, it makes sense that eventually there would be a tendency to treat them more harshly. One way to stop this is to stay out of trouble, but that's hard to do when so many black spokespeople are constantly laying the blame on someone else. As we discover who they are blaming and why, we'll be in better shape to reach a solution.

BEYOND THE TALK

There are watchdog groups in this area that stage situations to determine if racial discrimination is evident. One thing that they do is to have a white couple and a black couple with similar education and credit records apply for a vacancy at an apartment complex. According to their reports, the majority of the vacancies went to whites. This is considered racial discrimination, with no consideration being given to the white apartment complex manager.

The white manager may be aware of the "us against them" attitude held by blacks, as most of us are and as black spokespeople confirm on a daily basis. The manager might also be aware of a higher crime rate among blacks, including rapes, robbery, and murder, which might make the manager consider black tenants to be somewhat more of a risk. We are all individuals and should be treated as such, but blacks make that very difficult to do with the *divide, separate, and group* mentality that they have toward whites. It is very difficult to get diversity and inclusion when you practice dividing, separating, and grouping. Where's the inclusion in the "Stop Black on Black Crime" campaign? Is the idea behind this campaign that it is okay to go to a non-black neighborhood and commit crimes?

I recently ran across an article by Jonah Goldberg, titled "Diversity Means Discrimination Against Many Asian-Americans." In part his article, concerning college applicants, points to a study by two Princeton academics stating that if you got rid of racial preferences in higher education, the number of whites admitted to schools would remain fairly constant. However, without racial preferences, Asians would take roughly eighty percent of the positions now allotted to Hispanic and black students. In other words, there is a quota—though none dare call it that— keeping Asians out of elite schools in numbers disproportionate to their merit.

The article goes on to say that it is far from clear whether or not diversity is good for black students. Peter Kirsanow, a member of the US Commission on Civil Rights, notes that there is now ample empirical data showing that the supposed benefits of diversity in education are fleeting and often are simply nonexistent. Black students admitted to universities above their skill level often do poorly and fail to graduate in high numbers.

UCLA law professor Richard Sander found that nearly half of black law students reside in the bottom ten percent of their law school classes. If they went to schools one notch down, they might do far better. Kirsanow asks: "Would college administrators continue to mouth such platitudes about affirmative action if their students knew that preferential admissions cause black law students to flunk out at two and a half times the rate of whites? Or that black law students are six times less likely to pass the bar? Or that half of black law students never become lawyers?" But all this misses the point. Today's diversity doctrine was contrived as a means of making racial preferences permanent. Affirmative action was intended as a temporary remedy for the tragic mistreatment of African-Americans in the past. But as affirmative action drifted into racial preferences, it became constitutionally suspect. All racial preferences are discriminatory. If I give extra credit to Ken because he's black, I'm making things that much harder for Tom, because he's white.

The diversity doctrine avoids all of this by saying that diversity is not so much about helping the underprivileged as it is about providing a rich educational experience for everyone. When the University of Michigan's administration policies were reviewed by the Supreme Court, former school President Lee Bollinger explained that diversity was "as essential as the study of the Middle Ages, of international politics and of Shakespeare" because exposure to people of different hues lies at the core of the educational experience. Another way of saying this would be to say that racial preferences are forever, just like the timeless works of the immortal bard.

Redressing discrimination against blacks is no longer the name of the game. It's difficult to put into words how condescending this is. It renders black students into props; show-and-tell objects for the other kids' educational benefit. There was a time when condescension, discrimination, arrogant social engineering along racial lines, and the like were dubbed racism. To paraphrase Shakespeare, racism by any other name still stinks. What this article fails to note is that blacks don't care that affirmative action has a negative effect on other minorities, or even themselves. Regardless of these facts, many blacks want to leap in the direction of a free college education in the name of reparations.

The three main panel members of the JCCI study were Bruce Barcelo, a political consultant, Circuit Judge Brian J. Davis, and Ben Warner, who has since become Deputy Director of JCCI. In my opinion, these gentlemen did a fine job presiding over a study of such importance to not only the Jacksonville community but the entire country and one that sparks such raw emotion.

Having said that, one of the most troubling aspects of this experience came near the end of the study, and it got quite a bit of press from the *Florida Times Union*. In a front-page article, Bruce Barcelo was quoted as saying the study was "never about what people felt," which was something I had never heard before. In my opinion, feelings are what it was all about. How can you have a study that uses the phrase "improving race relations" and claim that it's not about how people feel? Anyone who attended knows that feelings were expressed throughout. Emotions are the root cause of present-day race relations between blacks and whites. Unfortunately most of these feelings are comprised of anger and negativity toward the other race. The theme of blacks not wanting to get along with whites is very constant and consistent.

On separate occasions, I asked two popular and well-respected black gentlemen, who frequented the JCCI study, if they knew of any black person with a public voice, locally or nationally, who encourages blacks to get along with whites on an ongoing and widespread basis. One of the gentlemen was Bryant Rollins, who is a public speaker and conducts seminars. The other was Reverend Pete Jackson, who, for a time, was the chief community officer of Mayor John Peyton's office, a position designed to oversee issues of race relations. Both of these gentlemen told me that yes, they themselves encourage such harmony. I've heard both of them speak publicly on numerous occasions, and I have never heard either one of them encourage blacks to strive for racial harmony with whites. Mr. Rollins is very passionate about the works of Dr. Martin Luther King Jr., often quoting parts of his speeches. But I've never heard him say, "Learn to love your white brothers and sisters; don't drink from the cup of bitterness and hate," or anything close to it. I was present at several meetings conducted by Mr. Rollins that were supposedly focusing on improving race relations, and yet I never once got the impression he had any interest in racial harmony.

One might ask, are there any white public speakers who encourage racial harmony with blacks? I can honestly say I don't know of any. But they also don't have the same responsibility, because whites aren't the ones setting the negative racial tone in this country. I believe that most American whites are not aware of the divide, separate, and group mentality of the African-American population. I do not think the general white population is obsessed with their skin color the way most blacks seem to be. Which attitude is better for America as a whole and humanity in general: to be obsessed with the color of your skin, 24 hours a day, seven days a week, in a negative manner or not to be? Many blacks even consider "skin tone" an issue.

Of course there are white hate groups that are not condoned, supported, or encouraged by the general white population. I would guess that there are millions of whites who are on the fence about racial division and who basically have good hearts and souls and harbor no grudges or ill will toward the African-American population. Others may lean in a negative direction because of the blame, shame, complain, protest, march, riot, boycott, and "litigate white people and the government" attitude held by the black population. These white people could easily be on the positive side of the fence if blacks stopped making everything a racial issue. Blacks are responsible for the majority of the discrimination and accusations of oppression that they claim. How could so many blacks who are doing so well be oppressed? Are we to believe that for all the blacks who aren't doing so well there aren't non-blacks who equal, and probably even outnumber, them in similar situations?

I think it is unlikely that blacks could get on nationally televised programs to make claims of oppression if they really were so horribly oppressed. One of many reasons that might cause the perception of discrimination and oppression is the use of poor language skills on the part of many blacks, some of which seems intentional. During the course of the JCCI study, I questioned the use of this altering of the English language and was told it is part of black culture. Doesn't it make sense that if an aspect of one's culture is hindering progress, in areas including education and employment, it should be changed? We are all taught the same alphabet and English from the same books. Choosing to incorrectly use the English language makes me think that these blacks are choosing to shoot themselves in the foot.

Recently I entered a convenience store and the only other people inside were two young black employees of the store. One was behind the counter and the other was stocking shelves. The one behind the counter said to the other one, "Why he say I lie?" I'm sure to be employed there they must have had at least a high school education or, at the very least, must have learned to read and write. So what is the point of speaking that way? Forget that one of them has apparently been accused of lying; how well can anyone expect to be treated in this world using those language skills? This is a good example of why some people are treated differently than others in our society.

I recall in the mid-70s, while employed as a radio personality in Daytona Beach, Florida, a fellow employee and good friend of mine, a black lady named Hazel Bynum, told me that when she was in college many of the black students were trying to learn Swahili so that whites couldn't understand what they were talking about. I can only imagine that Swahili must've been too difficult to conquer, so altering proper English was the next best thing. Either way, it shows a fairly strong desire to divide, separate, and group.

As the JCCI study went on, it became increasingly clear that actually discussing how to improve race relations was not going to happen. I felt I was the only one to approach the subject at all. As most of my input fell by the wayside, I decided to make my point in a different way. I decided to write an open letter to JCCI. I submitted an open letter in June of 2002, and I passed out copies to all the panel and committee members who were in attendance that day.

An Open Letter to JCCI

When discussing improving race relations, one thing is certain; we all bring our color (mine is white) and background to the exchange. In my mind, and to the best of my efforts, I am not speaking on behalf of white people, or, on behalf of black people or any other color of choice. I am doing my very best to focus on fairness. But we must realize fairness is a concept, so flexibility is needed from all.

After more than six months of attending JCCI's study, "Beyond the Talk: Improving Race Relations In Northeast Florida," and being the author and publisher of a book about a legendary black man, Jackie Wilson (which I describe as a labor of love) I have acquired a substantial amount of understanding and wisdom about race relations, especially between blacks and whites.

Quite sadly, and frankly, there is enormous room for improvement on the part of everyone. The good news is we are totally capable and equipped to achieve widespread racial harmony. Our problems are solvable, depending on the level of cooperation from everyone.

A deeper understanding of attitudes and feelings of races other than one's own, should top our list of priorities. Excessive team spirit within the races may be our biggest obstacle to overcome.

America has been attacked from beyond our borders. We are plagued by dreaded diseases, and grave environmental concerns. So if we are going to fight something as human beings, it shouldn't be between blacks and whites. Common sense dictates that racial harmony is the only way to go.

The true heart of the matter is that blacks are as good as whites; whites are as good as blacks. Blacks have strengths and weaknesses, just as whites have strengths and weaknesses. Let's share our strengths and lessen the weaknesses for the benefit of mankind and humanity, and go through life down the same path together, even if it means we have to widen the path. Don't you think we can put our minds together and widen the path, if that's all it takes?

Let's all approach race relations from the standpoint of being fair with one another. It should be the least we can do.

We've had the Civil War; we have Civil Rights, why can't we just be civil? Is being fair and civil with one another too much to ask? Unfortunately, for many the answer to that question is yes. However, it's a worthwhile goal to set and go after, as we keep a watchful eye and pointed finger to those that thrive on bitterness and hate.

To coin an under used phrase… "WWJD…What Would Jesus Do?"

Peace, fairness, understanding and sensitivity for all,

Doug Saint Carter

Considering all that had transpired in the JCCI study, it was no surprise that my open letter received very little response. I don't recall any black individuals responding to the letter at all, although there were a handful of white individuals who acknowledged it. Thankfully, their comments were encouraging and made the effort seem worthwhile, but not necessarily successful. Throughout the study I kept wondering why whites were the only ones being targeted for being responsible for the present-day state of race relations when almost all of the negative noise comes from blacks.

The *Florida Times-Union* seems to get a great deal of criticism when it comes to covering blacks in the media. As a daily subscriber to that newspaper, I fail to see the bias or unfairness to the black or African-American population. There are news stories about blacks, whites, and other races that cover the spectrum from good to bad. If the local chapter of the NAACP has a complaint (which it so often does), it usually makes the front page of the paper, even if it has little or no merit.

I recall being the only individual to raise the question, "What about the black media? What responsibility are they taking to be fair when it comes to race?" The largest black publication in northeast Florida, *The Florida Star*, is almost completely for, by, and about blacks. On the front page of every issue there is a pie chart that indicates crimes committed by race. These crimes include everything from murder, robbery, and rape to check fraud and deadbeat dads. Blacks and whites by far dominate the pie chart, with whites leading in crimes usually by about two percent. This only stands to reason, since the white population is much greater in Jacksonville than the black population. I almost feel embarrassed for this publication, because when it comes to serious crimes of violence, such as assaults, rapes, and murder, blacks take the lead. This pie chart is misleading and I can only wonder who's falling for it.

Another aspect of the black media I brought up at the meetings was the Tom Joyner morning show. It is a nationally syndicated radio show broadcast locally with big ratings. According to the host of the show, they have a national audience of seven million. Unfortunately, the show indulges itself in an "us against them" attitude. They even have a regular feature called "Hidden Racism," where blacks call in and describe circumstances or events where whites are taking advantage of blacks in subtle ways. It's done with a sense of humor, and little if anything I've heard has validity. The Tom Joyner morning show is by far the most racially biased radio program in America. Probably the worst racial comment I've ever heard on the radio came from that program. Sometime between the O. J. Simpson criminal trial and the civil trial, one of Tom Joyner's sidekicks, Sybil, said that Christopher Darden, the black prosecutor in the criminal trial, was an "Oreo" (meaning white on the inside and black on the outside) and "a brother that's not a brother." What kind of message is that to send to their seven million listeners? To me it sounds like the message is that any time a black person is accused of killing a white person, the entire black population should support the accused, regardless of the evidence. There's no hiding that racism.

I am sure that the Tom Joyner radio show is good for a

lot of people. At the same time, I believe that it is a major contributor to the racial attitude of division, separation, and grouping. To be fair, I've tuned into the show many times over the years and have enjoyed the music and the humor with the exception of the lopsided racial material. Speaking of which, on June 14, 2007, Flag Day, while rushing to be on time for an appointment and having just tuned in the Tom Joyner morning show, I heard Tom say he had Senator Hillary Clinton on the phone. His first question to her was, "We have an African-American candidate [Barack Obama]. Why should African-Americans vote for you?" As I was in a hurry not to be late for my meeting, there was no time to listen to the rest of the interview, but that was enough to observe Tom offering another example of racially dividing, separating, and grouping. That question insinuates that for blacks, skin color trumps everything.

From my point of view, one of the most troubling features on that show has been that of Tavis Smiley. The first time I recall seeing Tavis was several years ago on a cable TV news program, which unlike the Tom Joyner morning show has a larger white than black audience. What I saw was a young, intelligent, professional, clean-cut black man telling the worldwide audience that American black folks need to take more responsibility for themselves and stop blaming others. I thought, "Finally, a black man with a message that could point the country in the direction of racial harmony." But that is not the message he puts forth on the Tom Joyner morning show. I've heard him open his comments by saying, "Black folks are disenfranchised politically, socially, and economically." Any part of that comment that's not disingenuous is something that blacks are mostly responsible for. Disenfranchise means to deprive of right, especially voting: *to deprive a person or organization of a privilege, immunity, or legal right, especially the right to vote.* Blacks are not disenfranchised, in spite of their *divide, separate, and group* mentality. I get the impression that Tavis must have a staff that scours news sources coast to coast to find anything that can be called racism against blacks, so that he can continue to keep blacks in the "us against them" frame of mind. I've heard him tell the radio audience that if they are buying jewelry for gifts, don't go to a white jewelry store, go to a black one. The intention may not be boycotting, but there's not much difference.

Spokespeople like Tavis must have an agenda. He has found a niche and doesn't want to lose it. He is telling his black audience what they want to hear: that all their troubles can be traced to whites. If there were a large American effort to get along racially, what would happen to his book sales, personal appearances, money, and ego? One has to wonder, because from all I've heard, racial harmony is not what he is preaching.

When it comes to the radio industry, the Tom Joyner morning show is taking full advantage of Black Privilege. I've never heard a predominantly white-owned and operated radio station dwell on race relations anywhere close to that extent, especially in such a one-sided manner. If they eliminated all the racial references, it would be the shortest program on the air.

Tavis was scheduled to appear at the annual Black Expo here in Jacksonville in September of 2004, and a friend of mine, Deborah K. Thompson, who at that time was with the local African-American Chamber of Commerce, had arranged for me to meet with him. I knew I would be lucky to get just a few moments of his time. So I wrote a letter that I had planned to hand to him. Unfortunately, Tavis failed to make the appearance due to the threat of a hurricane warning. I had placed the letter in an unsealed envelope and wrote on the front, "Who's drinking from the Cup?"

HEYDAY PUBLISHING, Inc.

P. O. Box 8925 • Jacksonville, FL 32239

September 25, 2004

Tavis Smiley,
Dear Tavis,

Congratulations on all the work you've done for the betterment of the lives of many Americans. No doubt we're all a little better off thanks to your contributions.

Realizing how busy you are I'll get right to the point of this communication.

Whenever there is an opportunity for me to speak on race relations and I'm addressing white folks I like to say, "Learn to love your black brothers and sisters, don't drink from the cup of bitterness and hate." Do you know where that line comes from? With the exception of one word, which changes the meaning completely, it comes from a speech given by Dr. Martin Luther King Jr. He said, "Learn to love your white brothers and sisters, don't drink from the cup of bitterness and hate." I feel it's only fair someone should say it for blacks.

Dr. King had a dream of a colorblind society, as we continue to strive for that I would like to encourage a color kind society. Too many of us are drinking from the cup of bitterness and hate. There is a great deal of needless anger when it comes to American race relations, as you must know that anger first and foremost hurts the angry individuals. By the way, you'll be one of the first to know that the title of my new book is, "Drinking from the Cup?"

Tavis, at what point can someone like you and I sit down in the near future and discuss improving race relations between black and white Americans? For something like this I'm available anytime.

When it comes to race relations I'm about fairness, understanding and common sense. I'd be extremely happy if we could just use our common sense.

Sincerely,

Doug Saint Carter
Doug Saint Carter

BEYOND THE TALK

Although I congratulated Tavis in the first line of my letter for improving the lives of many Americans, it's my heartfelt belief that when it comes to racial harmony, the positive work he's done is far outweighed by the negative. I know Tavis has written several books, and I confess to not having read any of them, mainly because I have doubts that he is encouraging racial harmony. I know for certain he's never done it on any of the radio shows or television programs I have heard. Recently I saw Tavis interviewed on a television show where he described race relations as a race. He said that if all the races were lined up at the starting gate, all the gates for all the races except for blacks would open at the same time, and when all the other races were three-quarters of the way around the track, then the gate for blacks would open. He gave no example or explanation of what he was talking about, which seems to be common for many black spokespeople. These kinds of comments only give the African-American population the green light to continue resentment toward whites, which of course keeps people like Tavis in the spotlight and contributes greatly to the idea of dividing, separating, and grouping. Further evidence of this is that Tavis hosts a television program called "The Annual State of the Black Union." He might as well call it "The Us Against Them Show." While watching the show I never heard anything promoting racial harmony between blacks and whites.

On that same program I saw Harry Belafonte refer to President George W. Bush as a terrorist, which generated a loud and lingering applause from the predominantly black audience. Regardless of Harry Belafonte's explanation, it's ironic to me. In my efforts to improve race relations between blacks and whites, I've often thought of the negative attitude of the African-American population as a form of homegrown terrorism. Blacks are all about *divide, separate, and group* and "us against them," and of course in modern times blacks have proven to be the most violent race in America. As recently as the early to mid-90s there were threats from African-Americans of a race war in Northeast Florida, apparently generated by the acquittal of the police involved in the Rodney King beating.

On that same program, I believe it was Harry Belafonte who said that Dr. Martin Luther King Jr. said, during the civil rights era, he was afraid he was integrating blacks into a burning house. When asked what the people could do, Dr. King told them to become firemen. There was an implication that the house is still burning. But that fire has long since been doused. The general white population has matured greatly since the civil rights era, while the black population desperately hangs on to the worst of the past to justify needless anger. In the television interview with Tavis, he said he thought that Dr. Martin Luther King Jr. was the greatest American ever and that Dr. King told us that love conquers all. I keep wondering, at what point will Tavis apply that to his works? He obviously loves the niche he has conquered and the success it has brought him, but where is the love that would bring the black and white American populations closer to racial harmony?

With the help of Tavis and many other black spokespeople, an enormous segment of the American black population has the complaint department well covered. If it's not racism, it's institutional racism; if not that, it's discrimination; if not that, it's oppression, and of course, it could always be hidden racism. It's been said that "-ism" stands for I, self, me, which seems to apply to blacks here. Just like you, and everyone else, I don't have all the answers to improving race relations, so maybe I'm wrong or missing something about Tavis Smiley. I hope so. But even the title of his TV show, the "Annual State of the Black Union," has such a negative ring to it, especially if you're not black.

It was encouraging to learn that Democratic presidential candidate Barack Obama passed on an invitation to speak at the annual "State of the Black Union" program in 2008.

Democratic candidate Hillary Clinton accepted her invitation. I haven't heard what she had to say, but it's a safe bet she didn't place any onus on the black population for the negative state of black and white race relations.

Mr. Smiley not only uses, but overuses, the term "Black America" greatly. It's used in the title of some of his books. What other ethnicity in America does that? Not whites, Hispanics, Latinos, Asians, Native Americans, or anyone else. By using the term "Black America" so much, Tavis Smiley is propagating and preserving a divisive attitude.

What if all ethnicities in America followed suit? Nothing good could possibly come out of that, so how can it be good for blacks? He frequently refers to the gap between blacks and whites, stating that blacks are last hired, first fired, while never giving any examples. Who is really to blame for that, the employer or the employee? In a free society, with equal rights, that's something that should be looked at on an individual basis, not a blanket statement based on skin color. He also claims that blacks are the largest segment in America living near toxic waste dumps. No matter how unfortunate that may be, it's still a matter of class, not race. With Mr. Smiley extensively harping on the term "Black America" as we round out the first decade of the 21st century, improving race relations is severely hamstrung. But then again, improving race relations doesn't seem to be part of his agenda anyway.

Toward the end of the JCCI study came the findings, conclusions, and recommendations section. Since my reason for taking part in the study was to improve race relations between blacks and whites, my recommendations were a bit different than most, if not all, of the other committee members. I submitted my recommendations in print and handed them out to the panel and committee members. The following is a copy of those recommendations.

Recommendations for the JCCI study, Beyond the Talk: Improving Race Relations in Northeast Florida;

1. Create a policy that would have all churches in Jacksonville take time every Sunday, or every service, to encourage their congregation to strive for racial harmony. This policy should also be presented to local school systems, especially at the elementary level.

2. Recommend that all individuals in Jacksonville, and every city in America, be more understanding and sensitive to the feelings and attitudes of other races, especially blacks and whites. The room for improvement in this area is enormous.

3. I recommend that JCCI alert radio station WSOL/V101.5 that it has been mentioned more than once during the course of this study that their Tom Joyner morning show is without a doubt the most racially biased radio show in Jacksonville, and all of America. When it comes to race relations, they offer very little, if any, balance. Without it how can there be growth in racial harmony?

4. As a white participant of this study, I would like to recommend that any black participant or participants offer a recommendation that would encourage blacks to strive for racial harmony, especially with whites, on an ongoing basis, and broad scale. This gesture could dramatically reduce racial divisions.

5. Since race affects each and every one of us in this community, and all of America from the moment we are born until the day we're gone, all participants of this study, including the three panel members, should be asked to voice their views and opinions on this study to improve race relations.

6. Due to the importance of improving race relations, this study should continue indefinitely. If not through JCCI, then through some other forum.

Let's remember a comment from one of our guest speakers...WWJD...What Would Jesus Do? Let's try to keep that in mind at all times.

Doug Saint Carter

Referring to recommendation number three, I'm the only one who brought up the Tom Joyner morning show, which never received any discussion, probably because no whites, other than myself, in attendance listened to that show, and blacks seem to take endless negative racial chatter like his for granted.

It was also my intention to recommend that blacks and whites and all Americans stop using the N-word. Since the study, as it turned out, had little or nothing to do with improving race relations, I regretfully decided not to go there. A few years after this study, white radio personality Don Imus, comedian Michael Richards, and TV reality show bounty hunter Dewayne "Dog" Chapman all made racial slurs that brought national attention to this kind of language and efforts to eliminate it.

The only one of my recommendations that was supported by other committee members was number six. Many of us agreed the study to improve race relations should continue in one form or another. None of the final recommendations had anything to do with blacks and whites getting along with one another. Most of the actual recommendations dealt with the local government, including the mayor's office, the Duval County public school system, the Jacksonville Economic Development Commission, all public contracting entities, the Jacksonville Housing Authority, the Jacksonville Human Rights commission, the Northeast Florida Board of Realtors, the Duval County Health Department, the Jacksonville Sheriff's Office, the Supervisor of Elections, the United Way of Northeast Florida, the Jacksonville branch of the National Conference for Community and Justice (NCCJ), the *Florida Times-Union,* and others. All 26 of the recommendations can be found at the JCCI Web site, which is http://www.jcci.org.

All of the recommendations were designed to improve the quality of life for residents of the Jacksonville community, especially those in the low income bracket or at the poverty level. Even though to date most of these recommendations have been successfully addressed, the poor state of race relations has not changed, and it never will until black folks realize it's the right thing to do. All the recommendations were primarily aimed at improving the life of the African-American population. From what I could tell most, if not all, of the recommendations had to do much more with class than race relations.

Unfortunately, blacks seem to have convinced themselves that a negative attitude gets positive results. The non-stop blaming of whites for all their problems reminds me of the childhood story of the little boy who cried wolf. The little boy lived in a village surrounded by a huge forest, and every evening on his way home from school at the edge of the forest he would cry, "Wolf, wolf, help, wolf!" And all the townspeople would come running to help him. When the townspeople got there and found there was no wolf, the little boy would laugh and laugh. The little boy was having so much fun teasing the townspeople that he did this several times, until finally, one evening the little boy came to the edge of the forest and found himself face to face with a big, mean, ugly wolf, and the little boy cried at the top of his lungs, "Help, wolf! Help, wolf!" but nobody came to help. The little boy was devoured by the mean, ugly wolf.

Just about everything blacks claim is racism happens to everybody else too. Most of these claims can be traced to needless anger, which in the long run is more detrimental to the claimant than the accused. An article in the *Akron (Ohio) Beacon Journal* states, "The Poor. Working poor. Middle class. Wealthy. It doesn't seem to matter. African-Americans, on average, die younger than whites, regardless of the money they make or the neighborhood in which they live. In poorer neighborhoods of Summit County, Ohio, whites live almost three years longer than blacks. In more well-to-do neighborhoods, this gap grows into a chasm: Whites live to an average age of 76.4, compared with just 67.1 for blacks. That's a difference of 9.3 years."

Nearly a decade of life, gone. "I think it's the new civil rights struggle," said University of Dayton law professor Vernellia Randall. African-Americans lag behind on nearly every health indicator, including life expectancy, death rates, infant mortality, low birth-weight rates, and disease rates. "We have shorter lives. We are quite literally dying from being black." It's an ugly truth across the United States, where a black baby born in 2003 can expect to live 72.7 years, while a white baby is expected to live to be 78.

American Indians and Alaska natives have an even bleaker life expectancy than blacks: 70.6 years. And at the other end of the life spectrum, a newborn Asian-American girl can be expected to live the longest, until 85.8. There's no simple reason for these disparities, but rather a complex set of social, economic, educational, cultural, and racial circumstances. A lack of health insurance, a distrust of the medical establishment, poor personal choices, and inferior health care are all factors. Of all the indignities African-Americans have confronted in this nation's history—from slavery to segregation to inequality in housing, education, and income—the health gap is one that has remained virtually unchanged.

A 2005 report by former US Surgeon General David Satcher found that in 2002, African-Americans suffered 40.5% more deaths—a total of 83,750 more—than they would have if they shared the same mortality rate as whites. Anyone who thinks that carrying the eternal flame of needless anger toward whites isn't a major factor in these statistics knows very little about black and white American race relations. Stress kills.

Another observed consistency about the black population, both locally and nationally, is that because blacks are a minority they can't be racist. This seems to be another circumstance where blacks have gone to great effort to convince themselves of something false. It allows them to have a racist attitude toward whites, while claiming exemption based on their minority status. By definition, anyone can be a racist. It's a matter of thought process or attitude by an individual or group of individuals that anyone can have. The first definition of racism as described in a dictionary is: *a belief or doctrine that inherent differences among the various human races determine cultural or individual achievement, usually involving the idea that one's own race is superior and has the right to rule others.* By this definition, racism is not the burden of any race in particular because a belief is something anyone can have. There is no modern-day doctrine, as described in part one of the definition.

The second definition is: *a policy, system of government, etc. based upon or fostering such doctrine; discrimination.* There is no policy or system of government in the United States of America fostering such a doctrine.

The third definition is: *hatred or intolerance of another*

race or other races. Hatred is not exclusive to a particular color of skin or ethnicity, and neither is intolerance.

All the pieces of this definition can be applied to a person of any race. The term racist or racism is used far too often in American dialogue. Just because you dislike someone of another race doesn't automatically qualify you as a racist, even if you are a member of the majority and the other is a minority. Of course there are racists among us, and far too many at that. But it is a learned behavior; we aren't born racist. Furthermore, Eleanor Roosevelt was quoted as saying, "No one can make you feel inferior without your consent."

The term "white privilege" is also used a great deal in the litany of never-ending complaints by blacks as a way to inflict white guilt. The definition of privilege is: *restricted right or benefit: an advantage, right, or benefit that is not available to everyone.* By law we all have equal rights. As far as advantage is concerned, there has always been and there will always be advantages and disadvantages within the human race. It is my opinion and observation that the divide, separate, and group attitude of the black population ultimately creates disadvantages. There are probably more policies and programs in effect specifically designed to help members of the minority populations than most people are aware of.

In attendance at the JCCI study were a couple of members of the NAAWP, the National Association for the Advancement of White People. While their basic views are not shared by the general white population, the general consensus of why they were in attendance was agreed upon by many of the committee members, including some blacks, which was that discrimination in any form is still discrimination. For example, hiring blacks who are less qualified than whites for a position is discrimination. So is giving scholarships to minorities simply to meet a quota rather than selecting the most deserving. Thankfully I haven't heard anyone crying, "Black privilege!" which, by the way, seems to fit the definition much more accurately than the claim of white privilege.

One story out of Charleston, South Carolina sounds a lot like an attempt to exercise black privilege. A federal court has ruled that a white teacher in a predominantly African-American school was subjected to a racially hostile workplace. The case was about a teacher, Elizabeth Kandrac, who was verbally abused by black students at Brentwood Middle School on a regular basis. Regardless of frequent complaints, school officials did nothing to intervene on the teacher's behalf, arguing that the racially charged profanity was simply part of the student's culture. If Kandrac couldn't handle the cursing, school officials told her, she was in the wrong school.

After losing her job over the issue, Kandrac eventually filed a complaint with the Equal Employment Opportunity Commission and subsequently brought a lawsuit against the Charleston County School District, the school's principal, and an associate superintendent. Last fall (2006), jurors found that the school was a racially hostile environment to teach in and that the school district had retaliated against the teacher for complaining about it. The defendants sought a new trial, but US District Judge David C. Norton recently affirmed the verdict. The school district and Kandrac settled for $200,000.

The larger issue for students, parents, and society is the idea that a particular group of people can be allowed to behave in a grossly uncivil and threatening way by virtue of their racial "culture." An important legal question was whether a school could be responsible for students' behavior. The black children of Brentwood had been given a pass for their behavior, because vulgar language was considered normal for their culture.

What these students called the teacher is beyond reprehensible and could only be construed as hostile and threatening. A number of white teachers and students corroborated Kandrac's experience, including a male war veteran, who testified he would rather return to Vietnam than to Brentwood. Kandrac's attorney, Larry Kobrovsky, argued that the repetitive use of the word "white" made the slurs racist in nature. But school officials insisted that because black students were equally abusive to other blacks, the language wasn't inherently racist.

I am certain that if the black and white racial component of this story were reversed, and white students had used similar language toward black students and teachers, the story would have been headlines all across the country, and loss of employment inevitable. But since the Reverends Jackson and Sharpton would find it difficult to defend these black students, and weren't about to defend this white teacher, their absence is duly noted. Because the white teacher faced a daily onslaught of insults, had books and desks thrown at her, her bicycle tires punctured, and complained about it, she lost her job. Looks like when it comes to civil rights, America's black spokespeople seem to lack diversity and inclusion.

Throughout the JCCI study I would ask, "What efforts are blacks putting forth to improve race relations?" The response was always silence, but the need is deafening.

Chapter 4
WHAT JUST HAPPENED?

As the JCCI study was coming to a close, I began to feel a sense of anxiety because it felt as though nothing had been accomplished. Worse yet, there was no evidence of any effort to do so. While desperately wanting to continue this quest in a process that really wasn't even taking place, I signed up to attend the "Study Circles." These circles were small groups of five to maybe 15 people of different races coming together to discuss race relations, mainly focusing on issues between blacks and whites. One thing I noticed in the beginning was that there was no claim or mention of this study's intention to improve race relations. As far as I could tell, it lived up to that negligence. What transpired throughout the course of this study circle was more or less a continuation of what I had experienced in the JCCI study.

Meetings were held once a week for about five weeks. Each meeting lasted about two hours, and usually had two facilitators, one black and one white. This particular group consisted of about four blacks and four whites. The facilitators were supposed to take a neutral role in these discussions. The black facilitator of my group was a nice lady who did a very good job of keeping everyone involved. Even so, she had no problem expressing her views and opinions concerning her experiences involving race. One example she gave as something that upset her greatly was when a white individual on an elevator mentioned that she spoke very eloquently. This offended her because she had no doubt it was intended to be an insult.

When I told her that it was probably meant to be a compliment—that it is common for whites to hear blacks butchering the English language and her good grammar may have stood out as very noticeable and that it may have just been her perception that it was an insult—she was insistent that it was reality and not a perception, end of discussion. Another seemingly frivolous complaint came from another black lady in the group. Recently the city of Jacksonville had renamed the 20th Street Expressway the MLK Jr. Parkway. Her complaint was that they didn't refer to Dr. Martin Luther King, Jr. as Doctor on the sign. On a rare bright note, a black gentleman in the group said it didn't bother him. But complaints such as that remind me of an old saying that if you sling enough mud on the wall, some of it is bound to stick.

At one of the meetings, the white facilitator brought in recordings of former slaves telling stories of their lives and experiences. I knew at that point that any meaningful efforts to encourage racial harmony were slipping away. In discussing slavery, the discussion is always from the standpoint of blacks, with no thought or consideration given to any other point of view. One aspect that I feel needs to be brought up more often is that mankind has proven that it can do the most terrible things to one another. Skin color acts as an equalizer, meaning that any individual black has the capability to be as abusive or violent or cruel as any individual white. Blacks are no better than whites, even though some white individuals took advantage of blacks for the purpose of free labor. It's not like the entire white population was involved. As a matter of fact, the vast majority of whites were not involved in slavery. So all of the present-day whites who have fallen prey to white guilt are contributing to the *divide, separate, and group* efforts of blacks.

Even though most white Americans were not involved in slavery, by listening to what blacks had to say in the study groups, workshops, task forces, etc., you get the impression that the entire present-day white population should be held accountable for slavery. Around the fourth week of the five-week study circle program, I handed out copies of my open letter to JCCI. As usual, there was very little feedback, with only one response to the letter. At last, a member of the black population came forth with a positive response. Amazingly, it was the African-American lady who had complained about the (Dr.) MLK, Jr. Parkway sign. This lady was very opinionated on many aspects of race relations. In my letter I stated that we are totally capable and equipped to achieve widespread racial harmony, and that our problems are solvable, depending on everyone's level of cooperation. After the study circles program concluded, we continued to communicate by e-mail for quite some time. She was very supportive of my efforts to improve race relations.

Do I believe we can achieve racial harmony? Yes, I think it is possible, especially when you consider that it is all a matter of attitude, which every individual has control over. I've been told that my solutions of fairness, understanding, and common sense are too simple to work. Some of the biggest problems ever faced turned out to have simple solutions. We can achieve racial harmony if we really want to. It is so simple we could do it overnight, but that's not likely to happen. Of course, the alternative is to continue to allow our hate, bitterness, and grudges to control us, while we succumb to the heart attacks, strokes, and cancer that such stress creates. Once again, to get the ball rolling, blacks must participate.

Near the end of the JCCI study and into the study circles, something became rather obvious. A very large portion of the African-American population is willingly victimizing itself. This portion of the black population seems proud of this self-victimization, which only further supports a division between races. We really shouldn't need an incentive to get along with one another, but there are plenty of good reasons to make it happen. One of the first reasons that comes to my mind is that there is a chance that the Al Qaeda or any other terrorist organization could use America's racial divide to their advantage. According to some news reports, there may have already been an attempt to use minorities for this purpose. According to a *Washington Post* story in June of 2006, federal authorities filed charges against seven men they describe as "a homegrown terrorist cell" that planned to blow up Chicago's Sears Tower and other buildings. But officials conceded that the group never had contact with Al Qaeda or other terrorist groups, and had not acquired any explosives. This was a sting operation known as the Miami Seven, consisting of five Haitians born in America and two Haitian immigrants.

During the course of the study circles, there was a significant amount of dialogue about the state of our black and white relations. I found it nothing short of amazing how the blacks present seemed determined to be insulted or offended by almost anything whites tried to contribute even when the intentions were good. Blacks seem to find some kind of solace with this mindset. From time to time I would hear blacks say they needed to heal or that they needed to start the healing process. To me, it seemed as though the real motive was to not only maintain the wounds but to nurture their festering.

One serious but solvable issue blacks need to deal with is that blacks don't want to be treated differently, and at the same time, blacks do want to be treated differently. Having it both ways is not rational thinking and will not work out in the end. A very frustrating aspect for me is that, no matter what kind of constructive criticism I offer to blacks, there is never any concession that they have any room for improvement. Blacks simply don't want any criticism from whites, and not much from other blacks. And yet, so many blacks have no problem blaming whites for just about anything that displeases them.

As far as the value of these study circles is concerned, I'm just not sure what good they have done. From what I have seen, it seems that they have only brought individuals of opposite races together to share their opinions about each other without much, if any, encouragement to strive for racial harmony. The mayor at the time, John Delaney, mentioned that the people who would benefit the most from this process would never take part in it. And I believe he's right about that. Equally as important is that if the blacks who participate in this process don't open their hearts and minds to the concept of change, then it is going to be a useless undertaking.

Relating to one another as individuals rather than as members of an opposing team would make things a lot better for everyone. As comedian and civil rights activist Dick Gregory says, if black people woke up tomorrow and there were no white people anywhere to be seen, they would still have the same problems they had yesterday. And if white people woke up tomorrow and there were no black people, they, too, would have the same problems they had yesterday.

I do not want to leave the impression that I think study circles are of no value. It is my understanding that many individuals of opposite races who take part in the process sometimes form relationships that continue on after the study circle program has concluded. Of course it's not all that unusual for black and white individuals to form positive and long-lasting relationships. The real problem lies with the widespread disregard for fairness, understanding, and common sense within the black population. While fairness is somewhat conceptual, understanding applies not just to whites, but also blacks. We need to consider the feelings of someone other than just ourselves if we truly want to improve race relations. Even if you find it to be exceedingly difficult to exercise fairness and understanding, the very least we should use is common sense, which has usually developed at the sixth grade level. The current state of American race relations indicates a serious lack of common sense. To quote the late Will Rogers, "Common sense ain't common."

Knowing there will be those of both the black and white races who will accuse me of painting the African-American population with a broad brush stroke and only focusing on the negative experiences I have encountered, I would like to say that as a self-proclaimed racial harmony activist, I feel like a one-man band with no bookings, hopelessly searching for any sign of reconciliation. More importantly, I have yet to encounter even one black individual who supports my reasoning about how getting along with one another is the smart way to go. This attitude toward these ideas is constantly reinforced by the many black spokespeople throughout this country. Although they don't actually preach against getting along with one another, the implication is undeniable. Some of these spokespeople, such as Louis Farrakhan, Malik Shabazz, and others are much more obvious. Those two actually seem like hate-filled foreign dictators promoting divisive beliefs.

Thankfully there are a few blacks in the media who condemn the eternal blame, shame, and complain attitudes that permeate black culture. While these few may not be campaigning for racial harmony, at least they are encouraging fairness, understanding, and common sense. In early 2003, Dr. Valveta Turner, from the Florida Community College in Jacksonville and a candidate for a City Council seat in District 9 whom I met during the JCCI study, invited me to speak during Black History Month about my Jackie Wilson book, which I was glad to do. I asked Valveta if I could include how my book became responsible for my involvement in black and white race relations, and she was fine with that. I gave the speech on February 13 to an audience of roughly 225 people, comprised almost entirely of African-American students. Entertainment writer Rick Grant covered the event for the weekly entertainment newspaper *Entertaining U Jacksonville*. The following is part of Rick Grant's article:

Doug Saint Carter wrote a book about the pop singer, Jackie Wilson titled *The Black Elvis- Jackie Wilson,* in which he chronicled the life and times of this forgotten superstar. Last Thursday, I covered the lecture on Jackie Wilson at FCCJ Downtown campus as part of the city's Black History Month events.

Doug was inspired to give this lecture to both inform the public about Jackie Wilson's life and to clear up some misunderstandings about Jackie's friendship with Elvis Presley, and why he was called the "Black Elvis." During Doug's book tours, and his e-mail correspondence, he encountered some negative racially biased comments from

WHAT JUST HAPPENED?

blacks about Jackie being a pawn of the white establishment, and another example of a black man's career having to be validated by whites. Doug found out that there was a misconception about Elvis stealing moves and performing style from Jackie Wilson. The title "Black Elvis" had inadvertently inflamed racial resentments from some African-Americans.

This puzzled and troubled Doug, who realized that there was still much work to be done to forge better race relations, which he cleverly integrated into his lecture. He told the FCCJ gathering that the truth was, Elvis Presley and Jackie Wilson admired each other, and were close friends. Elvis called himself the white Jackie Wilson and Wilson called himself the Black Elvis. Race was not an issue with Wilson's tag as the "Black Elvis." Doug volunteered his services to help the Jacksonville community improve race relations. Doug said the Jackie Wilson's story has evolved into a much bigger issue, in that, Doug saw his lecture on Jackie Wilson as an opportunity to offer constructive help rather than just talk about establishing better race relations in our community... Doug's lecture was an illuminating dissertation on an influential icon of rock 'n roll, and how the truth can heal the wounds of the past. As we inch closer to Dr. Martin Luther King Jr.'s dream—a colorblind society.

We're not there yet, but we're close. Doug is an example of how one person can make a difference. Imagine if we all get involved in erasing the past racial acrimony, to bring King's dream to full fruition.

At the conclusion of my speech, Dr. Gwen J. Chandler, Department Chair of the Downtown Campus Library at Florida Community College at Jacksonville and Dr. Valveta Turner presented me with a large framed memento commemorating my speech. Audience members were invited to enjoy a complimentary lunch in the college cafeteria.

Dr. Valveta Turner arranged for two large cakes as dessert for the occasion, one chocolate and the other a white cake, and both were decorated with the name Doug Saint Carter across the top, which I feel was the nicest gesture to come my way since being involved in race relations. It's my understanding that even four years after that event, it holds the unofficial record for the largest turnout for any guest speaker during Black History Month at Florida Community College Jacksonville. Of course it wouldn't be fair not to admit that promoting a video presentation featuring Jackie Wilson, "Mr. Excitement," was in large part responsible for the good attendance.

While I was attending the weekly study circle meetings, the JCCI staff was conducting meetings to form various task force groups. These meetings were much smaller in size than the ones held at the Southside Baptist Church over the previous nine months. These smaller meetings were held at the JCCI offices and consisted of a dozen or so individuals at each meeting. These task force groups were being formed to address the topics targeted for improvement. The targets came from the final 26 recommendations and included the involvement of the mayor's office, education, housing, health care, and a media task force, which I was a part of. It was my original understanding this group was called the "media task force to improve race relations." It was a small group that consisted of between six and seven attendees at each meeting, the majority of which were white. These meetings were held once a month in the offices of the local PBS television station, WJCT. I truly thought that this would be a great opportunity to make some real progress in the efforts to improve black and white race relations, considering the power of the media.

The co-chairs of this task force were Bryant Rollins, a black man from the JCCI meetings, and Bonnie Arnold Knight, a white lady. Bryant Rollins was the primary leader of this group. I think that JCCI must have requested him for this position, because I don't recall seeing him at any of the meetings where people chose which task force they wanted to be involved with. Seeing Mr. Rollins at the helm made me worry that my input wouldn't be valued, and unfortunately my suspicions ended up being correct. It's not like I wanted to take charge and run things. I would have been happy if I could have just posed a question to the media representatives: What responsibility are blacks taking to improve race relations with whites? Even if the answer was "nothing," at least it would shed some light on the subject and give the media a chance to speak from an angle they never seem to take.

The task force had a goal, which was to schedule a series of workshops for members of the local television, radio, and print media. Over a period of several months, we were able to put together a couple of these workshops. The first of these workshops had a pretty impressive turnout from the media; the second one was much smaller. To my astonishment, when I arrived for the first workshop I was asked, along with three or four other members of the task force, to sit outside of the room where the meeting was taking place. I was stunned, but none of the other ousted members seemed to mind at all.

During a break, members of the media asked why we were all sitting outside of the meeting. Since I had attended all of the planning sessions, and nothing was ever said about not being allowed to attend the workshop, it seemed to me that Mr. Rollins just didn't want to allow my input. As angered and upset as I was, I tried to be fair about the ordeal, and decided not to make an issue of it. Since it was the first workshop, maybe there was a good reason for it that I was unaware of.

After several more weeks of planning, a second workshop was scheduled, and just like the first time there was no discussion about any of us being barred from attending, but just like the first workshop, the same banishment occurred, except that this time only three of us were not allowed to attend. When I arrived, with a great deal of enthusiasm about attending this workshop, Mr. Rollins and Ms. Knight came up to me before it started and asked if I had received their e-mail (work had kept me out of the office, so I hadn't read the letter, which was a good thing in retrospect, because I'm sure it would have upset me greatly). They went on to explain that the e-mail stated I need not attend the workshop, but there would be a task force meeting following the workshop. Since I was already there, they asked me to sit in the hall again.

This time I stood my ground and asked for an explanation. What they told me was that they felt the need to provide confidentiality to the media representatives. I found this reasoning completely bogus. What were the members of the media expected to do? Spew racial hatred? Not likely, and no matter what they said, who was I or the other two task force members going to tell? This wasn't about confidentiality, it was about suppressing reality. I tried to explain to Mr. Rollins and Ms. Knight that my heart was in the right place and that I felt I was right on target with my point of view. Mr. Rollins didn't disagree with that, but it was his position that my motivation was purely ego. That also made no sense to me. Even if he were right, what difference would it make? If my intentions were to improve black and white race relations, then, ego or not, I was in accordance with the purpose of these workshops.

Ultimately Mr. Rollins avoided any serious discussions of my concerns or input.

As far as I could tell, the main thrust of what Mr. Rollins was trying to accomplish with the workshops was to get the print and television media to stop showing blacks in a negative light. This shift seemed to hinge on getting them to stop showing black individuals who were suspected of crimes, in handcuffs, being led to jail by the police. He showed no concern for anyone of another race in the same situation, just blacks. I think that true fairness would dictate either showing no one or showing everyone in that sort of position. I have personally seen many non-blacks (including whites) in handcuffs on their way to incarceration. This whole incident only served to convince me that my input was not welcomed by Mr. Rollins.

The task force seemed to get off track not long after these two workshops. The name was changed to the "Prism Project," describing itself as "Enhancing Cultural Sensitivity in the Media," which, as I mentioned, mostly meant not showing black suspects in newspapers or on television. The reason given for the name change was that we were going to take on other concerns of our community in addition to race. Naturally this made little sense to me since I felt we hadn't even scratched the surface of improving race relations. I mean, we ought to finish one project before moving on, right? Maybe everyone, except me, could tell it was a lost cause, and that's why they chose to abandon it. Mr. Rollin's attendance became less and less, and eventually the task force stopped meeting. I couldn't help but wonder if my point of view had in some way led to his disappearance.

The co-chair of the task force, Ms. Knight, always gave me the impression that she was worried our race relations dialogue would get serious and difficult. She seemed to hope we could always speak cordially—having nothing more than a light and breezy conversation with intermittent laughter. I couldn't agree more that remaining cordial is important, but beyond that, any type of exchange that seeks more to be polite than to get to the bottom of an issue will get us where we've always been—nowhere. If it is considered impolite or offensive to pose questions like the ones I did, asking blacks what they are contributing to the improvement of race relations, then we are endorsing the "us against them" attitude, an attitude completely devoid of fairness, understanding, and common sense.

At one of our regular monthly meetings (prior to the hall sitting incidents) several media representatives were invited to discuss putting together a compatible workshop schedule for members of the print and broadcast media. In addition to our regular task force members, there must have been about six or eight media members in attendance. One of our problems was not only coordinating a time and place for a large number of media members to meet due to their irregular work schedules, but also to convince upper management level members to attend.

At this particular meeting we used a large conference room at the WJCT TV office building and I was seated next to Mr. Rollins. When the content of the meeting got around to the subject matter of race relations that might be discussed at this workshop, I took the opportunity to ask the question to the media people in attendance if they ever considered the angle of what are blacks contributing to improving race relations with whites? The expression on their faces and a lack of response to the question spoke volumes. It was clear to me these media people didn't have the guts to tackle this question. Could it be they are afraid to rock the boat? Obviously they had probably never given any consideration to this angle of the subject. At this time, Mr. Rollins turned to me and quietly said, "There's a fury out there," meaning a great deal of anger existed within the local black population. My question is if we are serious about improving race relations, shouldn't we address this fury? It's my belief that most of this anger is misguided and needless. Exactly who is all this anger directed at? Is it the entire American white population or a select few? My educated guess is that for many it's white people in general. Posing this question is probably why I was banned from the two workshops that eventually took place.

One thing I have noticed is that with all complaints submitted by blacks, rarely if ever are names and circumstances given. That's the least that should be done. When complaints are detailed, action can be taken. For example, one complaint that was given to local TV station Channel 12 was that blacks were being discriminated against by trash collectors, who had stopped collecting trash in the morning and started collection in the afternoon, which left these trash receptacles vulnerable to vandalism or weather conditions that may cause trash to be strewn over their streets and yards. When the television station investigated this complaint, it turned out that the refuse collectors had just started alternating their pickups to afternoons for a week or a month, or whatever it was and then went back to mornings. Race had absolutely nothing to do with their changes. Another complaint, which turned out to be one more of class than race, was that when a murder took place in an affluent white area, the media wouldn't be standing in the victim's front yard with cameras and microphones as they would in less affluent black or white neighborhoods. As it turned out, according to a black lady attending this task force meeting, it was because whites could threaten the local TV stations with a lawsuit, while blacks can't afford attorneys. This seems to be a situation that concerns class as opposed to one of racism.

Since there is no such thing as a college degree in racial harmony or improving race relations, and no group or individual can be turned to for all the answers, we must take it upon ourselves to create better race relations in America. It seems there are more high school and college courses on African-American history that do more harm than good when it comes to racial harmony. Most of us, at one time or another, tend to speak degradingly about our fellow human beings, an activity I believe is rampant in America. We all have flaws to some degree. I confess to mine, and so should everyone else. If we all did that, the tolerance we need to improve race relations might be easier to discover.

During the time that the "Improving Race Relations Task Force" or "Prism Project" existed, we would usually discuss race-related stories that had recently made local news. The response to one story in particular, from a couple of our task force members (one black, one white), seemed to encapsulate the mainstream attitudes of blacks and whites in America. A front-page story in the *Florida Times-Union*, in February 2004, was about black US Representative Corrine Brown. The article said that Representative Brown (a Jacksonville resident) had verbally attacked a top Bush administration official during a Washington briefing on the crisis in Haiti. The article reported that Representative Brown had called the president's policy stance toward the beleaguered nation "racist" and called his representatives "a bunch of racist white men."

Her outburst was directed at Assistant Secretary of State Roger Noriega during a closed-door meeting on Capitol Hill. Noriega, a Mexican-American, is the State Department's top official for Latin America.

Brown sat directly across the table from Noriega and yelled into a microphone. Her comments sent a hush over the hour-long meeting, which was attended by about 30 people, including several members of Congress and Bush administration officials.

Noriega later told Brown: "As a Mexican-American, I deeply resent being called a racist, and branded a white man." According to three participants, Brown then told him, "You all look alike to me." She adamantly rejected any apology or second thoughts about her words: "Absolutely not. I just want to save the Haitian people." A short time later, Ms. Brown apologized, saying, "I sincerely did not mean to offend Secretary Noriega or anyone in the room. Rather, my comments, as they relate to 'white men,' were aimed at the policies of the Bush administration as they pertain to Haiti, which I do consider to be racist."

The response from a white lady in our task force was that we whites are so accustomed to these types of comments from Representative Brown that they just fly over our heads. A male black member of our task force responded to these comments by saying that Representative Brown's constituents expect these type of comments from her, and applaud them. I think Representative Brown's outburst, and the reaction of the two task force members, is telling, and exemplifies black and white attitudes common in America today. Whites are mostly apathetic, while blacks express and even condone animosity.

Another article that appeared in the *Times-Union*, in April of 2004, was titled "Life in the Murder Zone." "An area with one-tenth of the city's population has one-third of its murders, and hope is nearly lost." This north-side neighborhood has a large African-American population. The same black gentleman from the task force who commented on Representative Brown's statements said this article was hurtful and opened old wounds, which made me feel that he was trying to make whites feel guilty. This was a factual news story about a topic extremely important to our city as a whole. Whose wounds are more important here, those of the overly sensitive black man from the task force or those of the innocent victims who were killed? Pursuing the white guilt agenda is like leaving footprints in the sand; they make an impression but can't stand up to the test of time. Rather than discussing this issue and pursuing possible solutions, this individual of African-American descent chose to divert attention to his claim of pain, which of course is something for which I'm sure he wants everyone to believe whites are responsible.

The Jacksonville Human Rights Commission, which heads up the study circles, has another type of event called Action Forums. These are infrequently scheduled events for those individuals who attended the study circles and want to take it to another level. Having attended a couple of these forums, I found it was still evident that striving for racial harmony was not the main goal. But since my media task force had faded into the sunset, I thought I should give it a try, because I still wanted to pursue efforts to improve race relations between blacks and whites.

A rather large Action Forum was held at the WJCT TV station in mid-2005, with maybe 50 or 60 people (blacks and whites) in attendance. While various aspects of race relations were discussed, the main goal here was to divide up into task forces and pursue a particular aspect of race-related issues. I chose a group of about 12 or 15 people called the "Humanity Task Force." This turned out to be my worst experience yet in working to improve race relations. Although the original group of more than a dozen quickly dwindled down to no more than a handful, I stuck with it.

In attending these weekly meetings, once again, I was the only one trying to put the focus on the need to improve race relations. You would think a group calling itself the "Humanity Task Force" would be more responsive to my ideas, but it was not so. By the time the first, and to my knowledge, only workshop came about, there were only three blacks and two whites left. One white lady on this task force, like so many other white ladies I have met on this journey, supported and went along with whatever the blacks were trying to accomplish. And so far it's never been about improving race relations. The workshop designed by this task force was divided into three segments. The first one dealt with DNA research proving that we are all alike on the inside, making the statement that not one characteristic, trait, or even one gene distinguishes all the members of one so-called race from all the members of another so-called race. It's my belief that this comes as no surprise to the majority of Americans. But to make his point, the facilitator showed slides taken from a PBS television documentary about how white scientists in the 1800s claimed there was a biological difference between the races and that those descended from African ancestors were inferior to whites. These beliefs were accepted as facts for an extended period of time.

The second segment of this workshop was called concordance. The point made here was that skin color really is only skin deep. And most traits are inherited independently from one another. The genes influencing skin color have nothing to do with genes influencing hair form, eye shape, blood type, musical talent, athletic ability, or forms of intelligence. Knowing someone's skin color doesn't necessarily tell you anything else about him or her. As the brochure designed for this workshop states, most variation is within, not between, "races." Of the small amount of total human variation, 85% exists within any local population, be they Italian, Kurdish, Korean, or Cherokee. About 94% can be found within any continent. That means two random Koreans may be as genetically different as a Korean and an Italian.

The third and final segment of this workshop was titled Social Issues, stating that while race isn't biological, racism is still real. Race is a powerful social idea that gives people different access to opportunities and resources. Our government and social institutions have created advantages that disproportionately channel wealth, power, and resources to white people. This affects everyone, whether we are aware of it or not. The brochure goes on to state colorblindness will not end racism. Pretending race doesn't exist is not the same as creating equality. Race is more than stereotypes and individual prejudice. To combat racism, we need to identify and remedy social policies and institutional practices that give advantage to some groups at the expense of others.

Unfortunately, these policies and institutional practices were never defined. While I am aware of policies that are designed to assist minorities, I am not aware of any current policies designed to take advantage of minorities or to purposefully benefit whites. This workshop had nothing to do with racial harmony and actually seemed to be going in the opposite direction. At one of our weekly meetings I made the comment that this type of presentation, in my opinion, is designed to make white people feel guilty for being white and to give the green light to the African-American population to continue down the path of bitterness, hate, and grudges. When I queried as to why this task force offered nothing in the way of promoting racial harmony, I was told by the black man mostly responsible for the contents of this workshop that we need to look at where we have been before we know where we are going. It has been my experience for many years (decades) now that blacks have immersed themselves in their past. It's like constantly looking in your rearview mirror while driving your car; you're bound to be sorry sooner or later. My experience with this task force made me wish I had sat out in the hall.

About a year after my involvement in the "Humanity Task Force," I made a discovery that made the DNA portion of that presentation obsolete, and apparently was even back then. Police were searching for a serial killer who had murdered five women in Louisiana. Leads were turning cold. DNA analysis of tissue found at a crime scene did not match profiles in the FBI's database of DNA from known felons. Then investigators sent the tissue to a private lab in Sarasota, Florida, for further analysis. In a conference call in March of 2003 with the Louisiana investigators, Tony Frudakis, the founder and chief scientific officer of DNA Print Genomics, reported his lab's results: The suspect was a black male. The phone line fell silent. An eyewitness had described the suspect as white and, historically, few serial killers are black. When Frudakis was asked if he was sure, he replied: "I'm positive. You're wasting your time dragnetting Caucasians; your killer is African-American."

Investigators refocused their search and arrested the alleged killer, Derrick Todd Lee. The first reported successful use of DNA in the United States to provide clues about a suspect's ancestry has impressed experts. Tony Frudakis, PhD said, "Currently the ancestry test is of superior accuracy. We have blindly tested it on a very large number of samples (3,000), and so far we have yet to get one wrong."

So apparently, we're not all the same on the inside.

In the midst of all these meetings, workshops, forums, etc., on a pleasant Friday afternoon in May, I was leaving a business meeting in downtown Jacksonville, heading toward my car parked in front of the Federal Building on Forsyth Street. At a time when that area is usually bustling with foot traffic, I noticed no one else was around except a hot dog vendor near the corner. He was a slightly large black man in his mid-30s, and with all of my recent activities in race relations, something compelled me to ask him a question. I asked if he was into improving race relations, and he started walking toward me and asked me why I wanted to know. I replied, shouldn't we all be into improving race relations? He said yes. But it only took a matter of seconds to recognize by his accent he was not an American native. He was from Australia and had been living here for about seven years. This seemed like a good opportunity to see what a black man, who in appearance seemed to be African-American but was not, thought about American black and white relations. I found his answer interesting, and in some ways encouraging. He said it seemed to him that whites were just trying to go about their lives, while blacks were making trouble. That was not the first time that a black individual not originally from America has said they don't feel like they are discriminated against by whites. It occurred to me that skin color may not be as much of a problem as attitude.

When I related this story to my study circle group, the African-American facilitator responded by saying, "They're not from here, so it doesn't mean anything," and quickly moved on to another topic. I, on the other hand, think it means a great deal, since African-Americans are obsessed with their skin color. Shouldn't stories like this prove that such an obsession is harmful and probably unnecessary?

The *Florida Times-Union* has a section called letters from readers, and a lot of those letters concern race relations. Recently one went like this:

Surely Dr. Martin Luther King Jr. must be rolling over in his grave when he sees the state of race relations in our country. No, not because black people are being oppressed, but because instead of his dream of people seeing and judging each other on character rather than color, most of the King wannabes, reporters, filmmakers, etc., see everything, and I mean everything, in terms of black-and-white. Only white people are expected to be colorblind.

No longer is it that goal to have equal opportunity for all. Now, the goal is special privileges and reverse discrimination. Any attempt to make laws uniform is seen as an attempt to keep the black person down, and inflammatory terms and images of slavery are dredged up yet again. Replacing one wrong with another is not an acceptable solution. Highly successful blacks who work within the system and don't incite protests are referred to as "Uncle Toms," instead of getting the credit they deserve.

Decades of equal education and affirmative action are not enough to allow people to be chosen based on merit. There must still be quotas or other exceptions. This is a real disservice to people of all colors.

Not only must blacks be fully integrated into all organizations and professions, but they must be allowed to have blacks-only versions of those same institutions in the name of pride. Some examples from the scores that exist are the National Black MBA Association, the National Association of Negro Musicians, Inc. and the National Black Child Development Institute. If white people try to do such a thing, somehow the same action is termed racist. Why aren't fully integrated organizations enough for everyone? Having separate ones only serves to keep people divided.

Dr. Martin Luther King, Jr. was a great man, with admirable goals I fully support. What I don't support are the antics of those who would love to be his "heir" or use his name for personal gain.

I would love to see a return of people working to make his original dream come true.

R.S. Murray

Unlike the Media Task Force, the study circles, and the Humanity Task Force, one group that came out of the Action Forum actually put their focus on improving race relations, although not necessarily just between blacks and whites. The Jacksonville Diversity Network or JDN, which formed in early 2005 and is still going strong, has been fairly successful. It is possible that this is because the man in charge of this group is neither black nor white, but Hispanic.

I attended a number of their monthly meetings early on,

and although the topics of discussions touched on more races than just black people and white people, when the topic was about those two groups, the results were no better than the other forums. I recall, at one particular meeting, the group was asked to express their feelings on reparations for African-Americans, and some of the responses were disappointing, to say the least. One black lady said she felt that all black people should get a free college education, and went on to say that there was nothing that could be done to make up for slavery. But if nothing can be done to make up for slavery, then why even try with reparations like the type she was suggesting? As I see it, nothing can be done to make up for slavery simply because it is so far in the past, it can have no bearing on the present state of inter-racial relations. But what the lady at the forum seemed to mean was that present-day whites should be held eternally responsible for slavery—which is something they have no responsibility for.

Another response, from a black man, was that black people should be given their own state. This is not the first time I have heard black people make that statement. Unfortunately, I assume that it would be useless to ask these two individuals what they themselves are doing to improve relations between black people and white people. I wouldn't be surprised if they waved a flag with DSG (Divide, Separate, and Group) on it.

The Jacksonville Diversity Network put a lot of focus on socializing, and paid a lot of attention to interracial dating (which of course is a personal preference). But at the very least they seemed to be sincere about improving race relations.

Chapter 5
IT CAN BE DONE

When we as human beings put our minds together, we can accomplish almost anything. While achieving racial harmony is an attainable goal, very little, if anything, is being done to move toward it. Evidence of this continues to pile up as my journey evolves. In working with various individuals of both races, I can truly say, for the most part, I liked almost everyone.

One individual I have great respect and admiration for is Deborah K. Thompson, an African-American who used to represent the First Coast African-American Chamber of Commerce as Vice President and Chief Operating Officer. Deborah and I seem to be able to discuss our racial differences without offending one another. For example, I started a conversation with her once about the fact that the name of the organization, the First Coast African-American Chamber of Commerce, made me wonder why there might be a need for such an organization. It's my understanding several cities around the country have such an organization, although I know for a fact that the Jacksonville Chamber of Commerce has many black members. As Deborah kindly explained to me, members of the black population were dissatisfied with the assistance they received from the regular Jacksonville Chamber of Commerce and decided to form their own. According to their Web site, their mission is "to create and promote programs and services which stimulate economic growth and development in the African-American business community in Jacksonville, and the First Coast region." Their vision, in part, is to create a viable, thriving, and profitable small business and commercial district on the north side of Jacksonville, owned and operated by African-Americans. My understanding, although not confirmed, is that these two chambers have put forth efforts to merge with one another, but so far have not done so. Merging together would be a great opportunity for both races to display a little desire for racial harmony, because as it stands I can't believe that there's still a need for a racially separated black Chamber of Commerce. There happens to also be a First Coast Hispanic Chamber of Commerce, which makes a little more sense to me, because of the language barrier.

Another organization that racially divides Jacksonville through an attempt to assist blacks is the Black Pages, a local phone book designed by, for, and about African-Americans. Most, and possibly all, of these businesses can be found in the traditional citywide phone books. I imagine that somewhere along the line, some black individuals were offended by the term "white pages."

There is an annual event held in Jacksonville and other cities called the Black Expo, which showcases a variety of African-American accomplishments, promotes local black businesses, and features nationally known speakers and entertainers. I have attended a number of these events and

IT CAN BE DONE

found them interesting and informative. A few years ago, the guest speaker was Spike Lee, whom I found to be very disappointing when it came to race relations because he is a clear-cut cheerleader when it comes to Divide, Separate, and Group. This was made perfectly clear when he said, "What if we were forty-three million strong?" meaning the African-American population, which got a big applause from the mostly black audience. Anyone who is interested in improving race relations might say, "What if we were three hundred million strong?" which, as a nation, we are, or would be if we could ever just get along! Spike Lee finds racism almost everywhere, even in instances too petty to mention. In one of his observations he said that in Major League baseball you never see blacks sitting on the bench. That if you're not good enough to start, then you're not wanted on the team. First of all, he's just wrong—there are blacks sitting on the bench in Major League baseball, although I'm sure that in his way of thinking, they are on the bench instead of playing just because they're black. With this kind of logic, almost anything can be called racism.

Like most black spokespeople, Spike Lee tells his audience what they want to hear: that whites can be blamed for most of what displeases them. In the small portion of his speech that was encouraging, at least to me, he did put down his fellow black people for such things as spending 250 dollars on a pair of sneakers. He also wondered aloud how it was possible that the language skills of African-Americans have actually gotten worse in the last ten or 15 years instead of better. Personally, it has been my suspicion that the deterioration of the language skills of black people, especially youths, has been intentional. Regardless of this shred of optimism, I have to say that when it comes to racial harmony, Spike Lee is doing a great job of keeping his fellow black people bamboozled.

So many black people, individually and as a group, claim everything that displeases them is due to racism, while white people, on the other hand, do little to challenge this assertion. One of many examples I could give of this broken dialectic happened a couple of years ago here in Jacksonville. There was a highly publicized murder case in which the suspect, a black man, was accused of murdering his ex-girlfriend and her baby, both of whom were black. It didn't take long for him to claim that the only reason he was arrested was because he was black. A few days after his arrest, a 15-year-old boy (also black) with a guilty conscience came forward and told police he had helped the suspect dispose of the bodies.

Accusations of racism by blacks have become commonplace, and too numerous to keep up with, but so many of the little things that blacks claim are expressions of racism happen to everyone. Who hasn't felt snubbed or mistreated by someone in the service industry from time to time? Whites get ignored, and receive unpleasant facial expressions from other whites in public situations—and this sort of occurrence has nothing to do with race. How could it? We all need to be more tolerant with one another, and more sensitive to the people we interact with, but we can't attribute all of this to racism. Sometimes the individual giving the unfriendly expression is not aware of it. Or else they could have any number of personal problems that cause their demeanor to appear unpleasant. Not that that's an excuse, but it is a possible explanation—one of many that have nothing to do with racial discrimination. If I go into a store to buy a pair of shoes and a black salesman hands me a box and a shoehorn, should I automatically consider that brusqueness to be racial in nature? That particular salesman may be paid by the hour or by the week, and does not get commission on the sale, so he doesn't care if I purchase the shoes or not.

In this day and age, truly having a color*blind* society doesn't seem realistic, but having a color *kind* society is something everyone can and should participate in.

Last year, between the Thanksgiving and Christmas holidays, I saw a couple of good examples of blacks falsely claiming racism on the A&E network reality TV show, "Airline." The show follows the exploits of Southwest Airlines passengers and airport employees at Los Angeles International and Chicago's Midway International. They were running a mini-marathon of their half-hour show, and these incidents occurred on separate episodes.

The first one involved a large black man, traveling with a black lady, whose relationship I don't recall. The black man became verbally and visibly upset, claiming that a white lady got in line in front of him. When airport personnel came to investigate, they attempted to calm him down without success as he continued to complain. When his complaint was investigated, it turned out the white lady was following instructions given by airport personnel, but this had no effect on the black man's attitude. He not only refused to calm down, he seemed to enjoy all the attention he was getting. The airport personnel assigned to deal with the situation was a small white lady who maintained her professionalism throughout the man's belligerent tirade. When airport officials decided to allow the white lady passenger to continue on with her trip and put the man on a later flight, he became even more upset. His argument at this point was not so much that he was being detained, but that the white lady was allowed to continue on her trip. It began to look like he was never going to calm down, and when he exhausted all of his arguments, he claimed racism. Anybody with common sense could see this man, regardless of his race, was behaving dangerously and should not be allowed to continue on that flight. The airlines had no choice but to conclude this man could put passengers and crew in harm's way and chose to book him on a later flight.

The second incident involved a black man whose traveling companions were a black lady and a black child. This man was obviously in a state of altered reality; he was either high on drugs or medication, or just plain drunk. Airport officials determined that he should not be allowed to board his designated flight and would be assigned a later flight. His traveling companions were allowed to take their originally scheduled flight and decided to do so. After pleading his case extensively without success, as a last resort he claimed he was a victim of racism.

I have seen many episodes of this program, but for those who have never seen this television show, these are the only two blacks I have seen prevented from taking their regularly scheduled flights, while I have seen many whites detained for similar reasons. And so far, no whites have ever claimed racism, even if the personnel were black (although, by definition, blacks can be as guilty of racism as anyone else).

Incidents such as these only reinforce the notion that black individuals themselves, due to unsociable behaviors, are responsible for a vast amount of the discrimination charges that are so frequently claimed. When claims of racial discrimination like the ones I witnessed on "Airline" are made, the individual seems to willfully ignore the fact that the behavior itself was socially unacceptable—and that anyone, regardless of race or looks, would have suffered the same consequences, especially in an airport post-September 11.

Another television show dealing with race aired in March and April of 2006. It was FX's reality show, "Black White." The hour-long show ran for six weeks and was a social experiment involving two families, one black and one white, who through makeup switched races and shared a single residence. Each family consisted of middle-class parents, with only one child.

The opinions of how this experiment worked are as varied as the people who watched it. To me it was a lot like my experiences of the JCCI study, the task forces, the forums, the study circles, etc., because improving race relations never got the attention it needed. As one critic pointed out, the white father, Bruno, saw racism as a non-issue, and the black father, Brian, saw racism as the only issue. It was true that both fathers seemed to enter the experiment with the attitude that proclaiming their own personal views was more important than listening to or learning from the members of the other race. On the other hand, the white mother, Carmen, and her daughter, Rose, appeared to be more willing to understand the other family's culture. The black mother, Renee, seemed extremely surprised that a white lady who didn't know she was black accepted her just the same when she found out the truth. The most encouraging individuals in the group turned out to be the youngsters, Nick and Rose, who were able to accept members of the other race as individuals without prejudging them. It's plain to see where some of our racial problems originate. While the black parents showed a great deal of concern that their son was getting along so well with the white kids, the white parents were fine with their daughter getting along with the black kids.

One thing I have learned in life is that many of society's biggest problems, including race relations, can be traced to bad or poor parenting. As the series came to an end, things between the black father and white father hadn't gotten much better, and needless anger permeated the atmosphere. As the show came to a conclusion, moods of the participants came off as friendly, and that the experiment was a positive one.

I don't know it to be a fact, but it seemed to me as though the show's producers had orchestrated a positive spin to leave the impression that things were better than they actually were.

In another video experience, I recently saw a documentary called *The N Word, Divided We Stand*, which was originally released in 2004, produced by Helena Echegoyen and directed by Todd Williams VI. The opinions expressed here were as different as images in a kaleidoscope. The participants consisted of celebrities, notables, and regular folks. One of the more interesting aspects of the documentary was that you could find black people at both ends of the spectrum. Some seemed content to wallow in their determination to use the "N" word while forbidding whites to use it. As far as that sentiment is concerned, it's just another example of divide, separate (segregate), and group. Thank goodness there are blacks who would like to see the word eliminated from social usage. Unfortunately, I don't imagine that is likely to happen anytime soon. Somehow over time, the word has acquired multiple definitions, and even different ways to pronounce it. If the word is pronounced "nigga," it takes on a more harmless connotation. It's more like calling someone a friend or a buddy or something along those lines, at least when spoken by blacks.

That's twice in a short period of time I have seen blacks putting or trying to put restrictions on whites. In the other example, a black man being interviewed on a cable television show was lobbying to ban white people from rap music, referring to whites in that industry as devils. When asked if he thought all white people were devils, he skirted the issue, leaving the impression that he did.

One of the more ironic examples came in late summer

or early fall of 2006 when the producers of the TV show "Survivor" announced they were going to divide the contestants by race: Asian, black, Hispanic, and white. Opinions were varied, but most of the interviews I saw around that time were opposed to it. White people, for the most part, were (I suspect) just trying to be politically correct in their thinking and said it was a bad idea. Some black people and white people didn't have a problem with it. The irony came from a black woman, whose name I didn't catch, who was standing outdoors in front of a microphone surrounded by a group of other black people in what looked like some kind of press conference stating that the show should be boycotted. I was surprised that she would oppose such a thing since the *divide, separate, and group* mentality seems to be so rampant within the African-American population. But then again, black people do seem to have a strange philosophy of integrating and segregating simultaneously. Maybe they're not thinking ahead, or about the big picture, and so whatever is beneficial at any given time is the direction taken. What worries me is that blacks are often trendsetters in America, which is evident in styles of music, attire, slang, hairstyles, which are all things whites have copied. Let's just hope white people don't pick up on the trend of *divide, separate, and group*!

One television show that deals with race in a humorous manner is the "Dave Chapelle Show," now canceled. His TV show is often taped on location, rather than in the studio. In one hilarious skit, Chapelle played a blind black man who was raised by white bigoted rednecks who never told him about his skin color; he even published a number of books about hating blacks. Here was a blind black man who hated all blacks, and he had never even seen one. Although it was a very funny skit, there is something more important that can be taken from it, which is that too many of us, blacks and whites alike, allow those around us to dictate how we see our fellow Americans rather than using our own judgment and making up our own minds about individuals within a particular race, rather than the entire race as a whole.

In 2006, the Jacksonville murder rate was much higher than usual, prompting JCCI to organize the "Reducing Violence Study." One of the first recommendations to come out of the study was to admit and address racism. Since I did not participate in this study, I don't know for a fact the origin of that recommendation. But an educated guess leads me to believe it was submitted by a member or members of the African-American population. It was never made clear who was supposed to admit and address racism.

The findings and recommendations of the study prompted a local resident to submit the following editorial comment to the *Florida Times-Union*:

Jacksonville's murder rate continues to rise, and frustration mounts as the community points fingers in every direction but the right one; political correctness forbids it, so we continue to ignore the source of all the problems—black culture.

Everybody loves Oprah, but the black middle class has fled to the suburbs leaving mostly poor black neighborhoods to scurrilous politicians who embrace the cult of victimization and the last crippling vestiges of slavery in order to promote themselves. Locally, Pat Lockett-Felder and Corrine Brown have carved out careers devoid of character that exploit the ignorance and poverty of their constituents for self-aggrandizement.

Clearly, we must end political correctness and start a frank discussion. No more wasted spending on yet another repetitive study that sweeps the real problem under the carpet and offers no solutions. The black culture that grew out of the 60s disrespects education, grammatical English, and has no sense of shame. It constantly demands respect. If not given, murder for minor slights is the result.

IT CAN BE DONE

We need to deal more honestly with the real problem and forget political correctness. Most murders occur within the black population. To stop it, we must really examine black culture. Real fathers are necessary to stop the killing, as most killers and victims are black men who never had one. The black population is desperate for leadership and honesty.

C. Stumin

Most of the anger within the African-American population goes back to slavery. At least that's the impression an attentive observer gets. I wonder how long this will last and to what degree blacks hold present-day whites responsible for slavery. For example, if white boy and girl twins are born in Florida's Duval County today and are being held by a black nurse, does that nurse hold those two newborns responsible for slavery right then and there? If not, when does it start? If so, and more importantly, when does it end?

This exemplifies the need for more understanding.

Local editorial writer Tonyaa Weathersbee continuously sees race, rather than class or culture, as responsible for many of today's problems. Her attitude generated this response from a *Times-Union* reader;

I must respond to Tonyaa Weathersbee's latest attempt to keep racism alive.

Her column, titled "Putting blacks in prison is the latest legacy of slavery," is somewhat misleading. She stated: "We're at a point in which we are incarcerating more people than ever before." Yes, we are incarcerating more people than ever before. But the incarceration rate, the percent of total population, has remained fairly stable for over 100 years. We just have more people today than in yesteryear.

Second, Weathersbee stated, "For black people, mass incarceration is becoming the fourth institutional barrier to progress for African-

Americans." While this may be true, it is the first self-imposed barrier. The people incarcerated chose, with the freedom of self-will, to ignore the laws of our society. Why they made that choice is influenced more by how they were raised than by any other influencing factor. If they are taught self-control at a young age, and that actions have consequences, then the incarceration rate will decline.

Third, the statement, "For black people, it is also fueled by sentencing disparities." She then compared white people with DUI convictions, which is an abuse of a legal substance, to blacks with drug convictions, which is abuse of an illegal substance. The alcohol abuse did not start out with a flagrant disregard for the law. The drug use was a disregard for the law from the moment it was first obtained. The comparison is invalid from a racial disparity viewpoint.

Fourth was the statement: "They don't fear prison or jail, nor do they believe they can avoid it."
They do not believe they can avoid jail because they have already determined that they are going to continue to defy the law. Judges do not incarcerate blacks, whites or any other ethnic group. They incarcerate criminals!

Finally this statement: "…that might mean the threat of imprisonment has lost its edge; that it's time to look for another way." This ignores the fact that prison is not the deterrent it used to be. It is not as difficult to bear as it was when prisoners were required to labor and sweat during their incarceration.

I do agree with her, that young black males (with positive character traits) need to get involved in solving the problem, in being a visible role model for kids to follow. But, until a home becomes a structured, loving environment the problem will only get worse. It is not a race issue; it is a culture issue. And the culture of the black population can only be changed from within the black population.

D. Hinman

In another story covered by Weathersbee, a Duval County jury deliberated only one hour before finding Thomas Bevel, an African-American, guilty of a February

2004 shooting spree that killed a Northside father and son and injured a woman. Bevel was convicted of two counts of first-degree murder and one count of attempted murder in the deaths of 32-year-old Garrick Stringfield and his 13-year-old son, Philip Sims, and the shooting of Stringfield's girlfriend. Bevel originally told police that two masked gunmen forced their way into Stringfield's home and shot Stringfield and Sims, but for some reason let Bevel go. Prosecutors played video recordings of police interrogations of Bevel that showed him confessing to the shootings.

In a response to her editorial on the case, Jacksonville corrections officer Kenneth Reinsch wrote in a letter to the *Florida Times-Union* that Tonyaa Weathersbee just does not get it.

In her column concerning the convicted murderer Thomas Bevel, I was stunned that she thinks it's "scary" that it took an act of violence for Bevel to find a sense of peace! She also finds it scary that there may be more like him on the street. It does not seem to be scary to Weathersbee that he is a convicted criminal who murders others, however. She wrote that he now has 14 real friends on Death Row. Be still my bleeding heart! Of course, he is among friends. He can understand other murderers, or as I'm sure he couldn't empathize with nonviolent people who, with hard work, honesty and education, do make it in our society.

Weathersbee would have us believe that society is responsible for Bevel becoming a criminal. She is right when she says that too many young black men are finding their comfort zone in prison when they ought to be finding it in their communities. Unfortunately, she either ignores or simply does not understand why this is the case. The reasons are simple: poor parenting, no education, music that teaches hate and disrespect, no skills, no desire to succeed, no respect for authority, no respect for themselves or others and few honest role models. These people, mostly young men, mock those who do succeed by honest means. In addition, they believe their failure is someone else's fault. Weathersbee should face reality.

A corrections officer probably has more insight to the

criminal element than an editorial writer with an agenda. Over the years, Tonyaa Weathersbee has left me with the impression that "Drinking From the Cup" is one of her favorite pastimes.

In mid-December of 2006, the annual JCCI report card stemming from the 2001 race relations study was released. From my observation it's difficult to tell who is more responsible for the prevailing negative race relations between blacks and whites in America, the media or African-Americans. It's almost a toss-up.

The article, on the front page of the *Florida Times-Union*, was titled "Whites and Blacks Alike See Racism on the Rise..." A report found racial disparities in health, politics, education and other areas. It said 78% of black respondents and 55% of white respondents cited racism is a problem. That represented an increase of 5% among blacks and 12% among whites over the previous year's findings. Those results were based on a survey conducted for JCCI by American Public Dialogue in September 2006.

Using information from a variety of public sources through 2005, the report identified racial disparities in five areas: education; employment and income; neighborhoods and housing; health, justice, and the legal system; and politics and civil engagement.

The report cited substantial progress from 2004 to 2005 in some quality-of-life measures, such as death from strokes, which were down significantly among both whites and blacks with a gap between the races having closed. Other areas showed progress for both races, but at uneven rates. An example was the unemployment rate, which declined among both races, but more dramatically among whites than blacks.

In other areas the report showed that "Jacksonville is slipping backwards." One discouraging example was the infant death rate, which was at 7.9 per 1,000 (up from 7.5) among whites, and 17.5 per 1,000 (up from 17.3) among blacks.

The report noted that home ownership had gone up among both black and white populations. The number of blacks buying homes increased 60% between 2004 and 2005, but this was accompanied by a troubling trend in which blacks had a harder time finding mortgages. As a result, 41% of blacks who purchased homes in 2005 relied on sub-prime loans at significantly higher interest rates. Because of the higher rates, there is an increased danger the borrowers could end up in foreclosure, the report noted.

To me the most troubling aspect of the report was the use of the term "racism," rather than speaking of disparities in class, which allows those already immersed in needless anger to feel justified in their negative attitude. However, it appears that progress was made in a number of areas for both blacks and whites. As far as blacks receiving sub-prime loans at higher interest rates, as usual, there was no explanation from lending institutions. No doubt many blacks believe those higher rates were based solely on skin color, rather than guidelines set forth by the banks that apply to everyone.

The report also failed to mention what white people meant in feeling racism is on the rise. Do they feel that blacks continue to pursue the attitude of dividing, separating, and grouping racially, or are they (whites) falling for the rhetoric that African-Americans in the media continue to pile on the American public?

Chapter 6
HURRICANES, RACE, AND POVERTY

In late August of 2005, when Hurricane Katrina slammed into southern Louisiana and Mississippi, devastating much of New Orleans and leaving so many destitute, dying, and homeless, I watched in horror and disbelief as the tragedy unfolded on television. But when I saw that so many of the individuals in peril were black, I knew beyond a shadow of a doubt that no matter what happened from that point on, many blacks and black spokespeople would make charges of racism. It was a natural disaster and unfortunately a natural reaction by that segment of our American population. Every level of government was caught unprepared for the storm—the worst natural disaster in our country's history, at least the worst that anyone living had ever seen. To claim that the poor response was due to racism reeks of unfairness.

One of the many racially motivated comments came from Grammy award-winning rapper and producer Kanye

West, who appeared live on a telethon simulcast on NBC, MSNBC, CNBC, and PAX for Hurricane Katrina victims. Participating celebrities were given scripts to follow, but West said, live and on the air,

> I hate the way they portray us in the media. You see a black family, it says, "They're looting." You see a white family, it says, "They're looking for food." And you know, it's been five days, waiting for federal help. Because most of the people are black. And even for me to complain about it, I would be a hypocrite because I've tried to turn away from the TV because it's too hard to watch. I've even been shopping before, even giving a donation, so now I'm calling my business manager right now, to see what is the biggest amount I can give, and just to imagine if I was down there, and those are my people down there. So anybody out there that wants to do anything that we can help—with the way America is set up to help the poor, the black people, the less well-off, as slow as possible. I mean, the Red Cross is doing everything they can. We already realize a lot of people that can help are at war right now, fighting another way—and they've given them permission to go down and shoot us!

West went on to say, "George Bush doesn't care about black people."

"Tonight's telecast was a live television event wrought with emotion," parent company NBC Universal said in a statement issued to the Reporters Who Cover Television after the broadcast. "Kanye West departed from the scripted comments that were prepared for him, and his opinions in no way represent the views of the networks. It would be most unfortunate if the efforts of the artists who participated tonight, and the generosity of millions of Americans who are helping those in need were overshadowed by one person's opinion."

West's comments would be cut from the West Coast feed, an NBC spokeswoman told the TV column (the Associated Press later reported that only his comment about the president was edited out). The show was live on the East Coast, with a several second delay; someone with his finger on the button was keeping an ear peeled in case someone uttered an obscenity but did not realize that West had gone off script, the spokeswoman said.

The sponsor of the event, the American Red Cross, also issued a statement on the telethon, stating: "During the telecast, a controversial comment was made by one of the celebrities. We would like the American public to know that our support is unwavering, regardless of political circumstances. We are a neutral and impartial organization, and support disaster victims across the country, regardless of race, class, color, or creed."

Black people comprised about two-thirds of the populations of New Orleans, and many lived below the poverty line.

Democratic National Committee Chairman Howard Dean said Americans have to face the "ugly truth" that race and class played a significant role in who lived and who died when Katrina swept across the Gulf Coast. Dean also said that "lots of people perished" because the Bush administration lacked "vision" in handling the disaster.

Several black leaders and groups have expressed outrage over rescue efforts. Among them was the Reverend Al Sharpton, who said that race played a role, and called Bush's response to the crisis "inexcusable." First Lady Laura Bush denounced critics who said race played a role in the federal government's slow response to victims of Hurricane Katrina, calling the accusations "disgusting, to be perfectly frank, because, of course, President Bush cares about everyone in our country, and I know that." Laura Bush told a journalist with American Urban Radio Networks on one of her flights to survey damage in Mississippi, "I mean, I'm the person who lives with him. I know what he is like, and I know what he thinks, and I know how he cares about people." The first lady also said: "I do think—and we all saw this—that poor people were more vulnerable. They live in poor neighborhoods; their neighborhoods were the ones that were more likely to flood, as we saw in New Orleans. Their housing was more vulnerable, and that's what we saw, and that's what we want to address in our country."

Secretary of State Condoleezza Rice, a highly educated black woman, is quoted as saying, "Nobody, especially the president, would have left people unattended on the basis of race." Whereas Jesse Jackson is quoted as saying, "Today I saw five thousand African-Americans desperate, perishing, dehydrated, babies dying. It looked like Africans in the hull of a slave ship. It was ugly."

It has been my understanding that President George W. Bush has provided more funding to assist the African-American population than any president before him. In the year prior to Hurricane Katrina, north Florida was buffeted by a number of hurricanes—Charlie, Francis, Ivan, and Jeanne. Almost exactly one year before Hurricane Katrina hit, northeast Florida's oldest and largest African-American owned newspaper, *The Florida Star*, had the following on the front page of its publication, under the heading of News In Brief; "The Hurricanes and Slave Ghosts":

It is rumored that the African slave ghosts are displaying dissatisfaction through the storms. The storms we experience begin from the coast of Africa and travel the routes that the slave ships traveled. It has also been noted that the storms are patronizing the heavily populated Republican areas of the US. Rather rumor or myth, Ivan has redeveloped, Hurricane Jeanne has shifted west closer to the Jacksonville area, Hurricane Karl has weakened, and Lisa is moving slowly out in the Atlantic. We don't know what's next, but certainly wish whatever it is arousing those slave ghosts will "straighten up" for we the living.

Any guess as to whom the "we" refers to? Even the softest gentle breeze, not to mention hurricane-force winds, is enough to blow the chip off the shoulders of many of America's black brothers and sisters.

Two months after Hurricane Katrina devastated New Orleans, Congresswoman Cynthia McKinney, D-GA read Homeland Security Secretary Michael Chertoff the headline: "Nursing Home Owners Charged in Deaths," about the case of 44 patients who were not evacuated in New Orleans. McKinney asked, "Mr. Secretary, if the nursing home owners are arrested for negligent homicide, why shouldn't you also be arrested for negligent homicide? It seems that chaos was the plan that was implemented. Leadership, Mr. Secretary, was lacking."

In December 2005, McKinney was still claiming that Katrina equaled racism. "Racism is something we don't like to talk about, but we have to acknowledge it," she said, "and the world saw the effects of American-style racism in the drama, as it was outplayed by the Katrina survivors." When it comes to race relations, Congresswoman McKinney is much more a part of the problem than the solution. When it comes to "drinking from the cup," the Congresswoman is a guzzler. Especially when you consider she allowed the New Black Panther Party to act as her bodyguard following an incident in Atlanta when she was accused of striking a white security guard. Members of Congress are not allowed to have bodyguards, and hers are about as anti-white as it gets in America.

One concerned citizen, James Fleming, responding to so much black criticism, wrote in part, "Certainly, while the likes of Jesse Jackson and other black spokespeople saw nothing but racism after Katrina, I asked, what about the millions of dollars raised in 'white' churches and in 'white' neighborhoods that were earmarked for those in need, regardless of color? Indeed, I never heard anyone mention the color of the recipients until the ugly charge of racism was raised by African-American 'leaders.' What of all the 'white' families that have without regard to race 'adopted' people from New Orleans to try and help them recover their dignity and sanity after such a disaster? When will we as whites have done enough to pay for the 'sin' of slavery and racism? Nearly seven trillion dollars have been spent, mostly unwisely, since President Lyndon Johnson started the War on Poverty to help the chronically poor. We have setasides and 'quotas' by whatever name you want to use to help even the playing field in employment and education."

In another Katrina-related story, on a weekend in May 2006, the Federal Emergency Management Agency (FEMA) and the city of Austin, along with the Texas Workforce Commission (TWC), set up a job fair for all the Katrina FEMA evacuees who had ended up in the Austin area. The job fair would offer information about training, interviews, and on-the-spot hiring. Several of the evacuees said that they had no transportation to get from the apartment complexes where they had been relocated. So the city of Austin, with FEMA and the TWC, set up transportation for each of them, to ensure they would be able to partake of the benefit of job searching. The transportation consisted of nine buses and vans, to run from four locations in Round Rock, and five locations in Austin, in continuing shuttles back and forth to the campus to ensure that the hundreds of people looking for jobs would be transported in comfort. The vehicles were brought to the residences, drivers knocked on the doors, and every effort was made.

At the end of the day, the nine vans and buses transported a total of one person. Not one person per bus—one person total. At the end of the day, none of the Katrina evacuees applied for any of the jobs. Not one person took employment—none total. The bill to FEMA was $7,800. After hearing about this story, I wondered if the Johnny Paycheck song, "Take This Job and Shove it," received increased air play during that weekend. It is inexplicable why these desperate people did not accept the help offered to them.

An article in the *Sunday Times*, published in September of 2005 by John McWhorter, makes the point that persistent black poverty is the result of 30 years of misguided welfare rather than racism. The article, in part, states, "As it quickly became clear that there was a certain demographic skew among the people stranded in New Orleans, journalists began intoning that Hurricane Katrina had stripped bare the continuing racial inequity in America."

The extent to which this racial inequality was hidden is unclear, actually. The fact that a tragic disproportion of black Americans are poor has been a hallmark of civic awareness among educated Americans for 40 years now. The problem is less a lack of awareness than a lack of understanding the causes for the persistent poverty. The publicity-sanctioned take is that "white supremacy" is why 80% of New Orleans' poor people are black. The civic lesson, we are to think, is that the civil rights revolution, like other revolutions of its era, left a job undone in an America still hostile to black advancement.

In fact, white America does remain morally culpable—but this is because white leftists in the late 1960s, in the name of enlightenment and benevolence, encouraged the worst in human nature among blacks, and even fostered it in legislation. The hordes of poor blacks stuck in the Superdome that fateful summer wound up there not because the racist white man barred them from doing better, but because certain tragically influential white men destroyed the fragile but lasting survival skills poor black communities had maintained since the end of slavery through the mismanagement of the welfare state.

There was a new sense that the disadvantages of being black gave one a pass on civility—or even achievement. This was when black teens started teasing black nerds for "acting white." Behavior that most of a black community would have condemned as counterproductive started to seem normal. Through the late 1960s, blacks burned down their own neighborhoods as gestures of being "fed up." But blacks had been "fed up" for centuries: why were these the first riots initiated by black rather than white thugs—while the economy was flush and employment opportunities were opening up as never before? The reason is that the culture had changed in ways that hindered many blacks from taking advantage of the civil rights revolution. Meanwhile, the most grievous result of the new consciousness was black American history's most under-reported event, the expansion of welfare. Previously, welfare had been a pittance intended for widows, unavailable as long as the father of one's children was able-bodied and accounted for, and granted for as little time as possible.

In 1966, however, a group of white academics in New York developed a plan to bring as many people onto the welfare rolls as possible. Across the country, poor people, especially blacks, were taught to apply to live on the dole even when they had been working for a living. By 1970 there were 169% more people on welfare nationwide than there had been in 1960.

This was the first time that anyone advocating for racial equality and civil rights had actually spread the message that black people ought to work *less*, instead of more. Politicians and bureaucrats jumped on the new opportunity for political patronage and votes, and welfare quickly became a program that essentially paid young women to have children.

Only in 1996 was welfare limited to five years and focused on training for work. But by then, generations of poor blacks had grown up in neighborhoods where there was no requirement that fathers support their children. Few grew up watching their primary parent work for a living. Most people paid only nominal subsidies for rent and were thus less inclined to treat their living spaces like cherished homes.

The multigenerational welfare family with grandmothers in their 40s became typical. Young women had babies in their teens, because there was no reason not to with welfare waiting to pick up the tab.

This is the hell that most of the people who ended up waiting for FEMA in the Superdome either lived in or knew at close hand, and none of them could avoid being stamped by it. Welfare reform was only nine years ago. The women now past the five-year cap are mostly struggling in dead-end jobs. This is better than living on the dole, of course. But these women are so weighed down by all the extra kids they created under the old regime that they don't have the time or the energy to get educated enough to progress beyond where they are right now. Poor black neighborhoods are not what they were at the height of the crack epidemic in the 1980s, but they are still a crying shame. The poor black America that welfare expansion created in 1966 is still with us, and today's poor young blacks have never known anything else. Even people in their 50s have only vague memories of life before it. For 30 years, the welfare state created a world within a world, as is made clear from how often the Katrina victims who were displaced to other cities mentioned that it was the first time they ever left New Orleans.

What Katrina stripped bare, but the media failed to comprehend, was not the long-term effects of white supremacy, but that culture matters—even if what created the culture was misguided benevolence on the part of whites. Social scientists neglect that before the 1960s poor blacks knew plenty of economic downturns, and plenty more racism.

But before the 1960s the kinds of behavior so common among the blacks stranded in the Superdome (possibly including multiple rapes) were fringe phenomena. Only after the 1960s did aberrant and antisocial behaviors become a community norm.

Wise people tell us that poor blacks in New Orleans went to rack and ruin when skilled industrial jobs left the city center, a common argument about declining cities nationwide. But in cities like Indianapolis where the factories largely stayed closed, the same degradation began starting in the late 1960s, simultaneous with the expansion of the welfare state. Wise people tell us that public housing projects destroyed poor black communities by concentrating too many poor people in one place. But in city after city, these projects were peaceful places until large numbers of welfare recipients were allowed to move in.

All indications are that the reform of welfare in 1966 is bearing fruit in terms of income and the life conditions of children. Hopefully, legions of poor black people who return to New Orleans will take advantage of the job opportunities that rebuilding a city will offer. But what we should all remember from Katrina is a tragic close-up of a group of people staggering from the effects of both a hideous natural disaster and, ultimately, an equally hideous sociological disaster of 40 years ago.

Darnell M. Hunt, head of African-American studies at UCLA, is quoted as saying, "You'd have to go back to slavery, or the burning of black towns, to find a comparable event that has affected black people this way." From another point of view, entertainer, actor, and activist Bill Cosby stood before 2,000 people in New Orleans and courageously said, "It's painful, but we can't cleanse ourselves unless we look at the wound... Ladies and gentlemen, you had the highest murder rate, unto each other, you were dealing drugs to each other, you were impregnating our thirteen-, twelve-, eleven-year-old children."

Colin Powell is quoted as saying, "It wasn't a racial thing—but poverty disproportionately affects African-Americans in this country. And it happened, because they were poor." The one group that was disproportionately affected by the storm appears to have been older adults. People 60 and older account for only about 15% of the population in the New Orleans area, but one database found that 74% of the dead were 60 or older. Nearly half were older than 75. Many of those were at nursing homes and hospitals, which is where nearly 20% of the victims were recovered.

Lack of transportation was assumed to be a key reason that many people stayed behind and died, but at many addresses where the dead were found, their cars remained in their driveways, flood-ruined symbols of fatal miscalculation.

Hurricanes will come and go, but "drinking from the cup" is all some people know.

Even two and a half years following the hurricane, many blacks still hold to the tunnel vision idea that race is the overriding factor. Where is the acknowledgment that many charitable whites have donated millions upon millions of dollars to help rebuild New Orleans?

So far I have yet to observe one black spokesperson offer praise to white movie actor Brad Pitt for undertaking a project to rebuild 150 homes in the Ninth Ward in New Orleans.

HURRICANES, RACE, AND POVERTY

Pitt's Make It Right project hopes to start construction by spring of 2008 and complete all 150 houses by autumn. The average cost of residences will be $150,000, and the foundation will coordinate no-interest loans to ensure that this price tag is capped at 30% of the deed-holder's income. To subsidize construction, Pitt and film producer Steve Bing have promised to match up to $10 million in donations. The pair is also seeking sponsorship of materials or houses via the Web site makeitrightnola.org.

Thank you, Brad Pitt, and the people involved in your project. You are great humanitarians.

BLACK HISTORY   AMERICAN HISTORY   ROCK & ROLL HISTORY

Doug Saint Carter Speaks At FCCJ

(Author of the book "The Black Elvis - Jackie Wilson")

Thursday, February 13th at 11:00 a.m. • Downtown Campus

You'll Hear The Music and See The Showmanship Of MR. EXCITEMENT!

Why isn't the King of Rock & Roll's Black Counterpart a household name too?

This Story Could And Should Be Used As A Catalyst To Improve Race Relations Between Black & Whites In America.

Sorry, no books will be available for sale or giveaway at this event.

Admission Is Free To The Public • Sponsored by the FCCJ Library
101 W. State St. - Auditorium Room 1068 • 633-8368

This is a print ad promoting a Black history month speech given at FCCJ in 2003. It's not easy getting booked to give a speech on improving black and white race relations. Blacks, for the most part, aren't interested, and whites, for the most part, seem either apathetic or are afraid of how blacks may react. So using my book on Jackie Wilson served as a great door opener.

FLORIDA
COMMUNITY
COLLEGE
AT JACKSONVILLE

May 13, 2004

To Whom It May Concern:

We at Florida Community College at Jacksonville were most fortunate to have Mr. Doug Saint Carter, author of The Black Elvis-Jackie Wilson speak during our Black History Month celebration February 13, 2003. Mr. Carter was well received by an audience who listened attentively and who were thoroughly entertained by hearing the story of one of America's legendary entertainment idols.

Mr. Carter distinguishes himself as a speaker by exploring within his talk issues designed to be a catalyst to improve race relations. Other topics covered in his speech are Black History, American History, and Rock & Roll History.

Again, we were very glad that Mr. Carter honored us with his appearance as he is committed to improving the knowledge and understanding of all.

Very truly yours,

Valveta L. Turner

Valveta B. Turner, Ed.D.

Dr. Valveta Turner of FCCJ and former City Council candidate for District 9 did a wonderful job of arranging a speaking engagement in 2003 which generated the largest turnout ever for a Black history month's speech at the college.

Dr. Valveta Turner and Dr. Gwen J. Chandler, City Council member and the Department Chair of the Downtown Campus Library of Florida Community College in Jacksonville, shown here presenting the author with a plaque commemorating a Black history month's speech on the Jackie Wilson story combined with a talk on the need for improvement of race relations between blacks and whites.

Sweet... Dr. Turner arranged for these cakes, symbolizing blacks and whites, to be shared by those attending a get-together, following the speaking event.

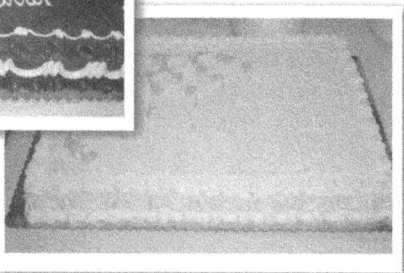

This print ad promotes a personal appearance by the author at a Juneteenth celebration in 2004. As with all events dealing with local race relations this was another disappointing experience. Action on the part of blacks to improve race relations with whites is nonexistent.

These are a couple of print ads which ran locally in Jacksonville between 2002 and 2005 which included encouragement for whites to improve race relations with blacks.

James Brown, "The Godfather of Soul" and Doug Saint Carter observing Memorial Day weekend, May 28, 2005 prior to a concert at Jacksonville's Metropolitan Park for the Spring Music Festival.

On December 30, 2006 during a nationally televised memorial service, Reverend Jesse Jackson made the comment that "James Brown's music crossed over, but he didn't." I'm not exactly sure what Jackson meant by that comment, but there's no doubt that it had nothing to do with encouraging racial harmony or improving race relations between blacks and whites. It sounded more like support for Dividing, Separating and Grouping. Jackson also mentioned that Augusta, Georgia, James Brown's hometown, was once a slave port.

I suppose that there is no chance that the Reverend Jesse Jackson could understand that the rationalization of harping on victimization is doing more harm than good to our Nation.

Chapter 7
BLACK SPOKESPEOPLE

To the best of my knowledge and observations none of the well and better-known black spokespeople, which include among others, Jesse Jackson, Al Sharpton, Maxine Waters, Tavis Smiley, Louis Farrakhan, Harry Belafonte, Spike Lee, Julian Bond, Andrew Young, as well as local and national members of the NAACP, ever encourage racial harmony or efforts to improve race relations with whites. Conjuring up racism at every opportunity keeps them in the spotlight they so desire.

In researching this chapter on black spokespeople I ran across a couple of articles by David Horowitz that warrant a close second look. The first one is titled, "Deafening Silence."

You probably don't remember the name "Ronald Taylor," and you probably think you have never heard of John Kroll or Joseph Healy or Emil Sanielevici. Why should you? The last three gentlemen were the white victims of a black killer, Ronald Taylor, in Wilkinsburg, Penn., just a couple of weeks ago. The story made the front pages for about a day.

BLACK SPOKESPEOPLE

And then, fairly suddenly, it disappeared from the nation's radar screen.

However, I bet you can identify Matthew Shepard, or James Byrd, or Buford Furrow or, for that matter, Tawana Brawley. These were the victims, the perpetrator, and the phony victim of politically correct crimes in which all the actors assumed roles that confirmed the prejudices of our liberal cities.

A DOUBLE STANDARD?

Taylor, a resident of subsidized housing, became angry at workers trying to fix the door of his apartment. "You're all white trash, racist pigs," he exploded. "You're dead." He then went on to randomly kill Kroll, Healy and Sanielevici, and critically wounded two other people before being stopped. When the FBI searched his apartment they found volumes of, anti-Asian, anti-Semitic, anti-Italian and anti-white hate literature.

But Taylor's crime did not confirm our nation's most protected racial prejudices, and therefore his criminal acts have been pushed so quickly out of sight. We get no Time and Newsweek cover stories about Taylor, no network features about black-against-white racism, no White House press conferences to berate the nation, no Capitol Hill resolutions authored by liberal Democratic Representatives like Barney Frank (Ma.) and Maxine Waters (Ca.) to condemn the outrage, and no calls for hate crime legislation that would specifically protect white males.

To these indicators, let me add a personal note. A few years ago I wrote a best-selling biography on the Kennedys, and my name is familiar enough to the media that every time a Kennedy kills himself, I get calls from a dozen shows to come on as an expert commentator. But even though I have a current book out called "Hating Whitey," which is rather high up on the Amazon.com bestseller list, I have yet to receive a single interview request to talk about this sort of hate whitey crime.

THE WHITE DEVIL MADE HIM DO IT

Even more striking, than the media blackout on the bizarre Taylor case are comments that have been voiced by the few black spokespeople who have acknowledged the racial discrimination of the crime. For example, Reverend Thelma C. Mitchell, pastor at the Wilkinsburg Baptist Church, told her congregation in a "healing" service:

"You cannot run from violence in the United States, because the United States was founded on violence. Why are we suddenly shocked, brothers and sisters? The whole concept of racism and prejudice and targeting people, this is not a new game. Although I in no way agree with the methods he used, I suspect Mr. Taylor really did reflect a growing frustration in this community, because too many African-American young men cannot find a meaningful job."

It's as if she's throwing up her hands and saying, oh well, the white devil made him do it. Far from being an extreme example, this kind of analysis is a mainstream excuse in the black population for the racially charged outrages committed by blacks. Dr. Alvin Poussaint, a Harvard professor, and one of the media's most quoted experts on the psychology of racism, is a case in point. Poussaint did identify Taylor's act as a case of "extreme racism." But in an interview with the Washington Times, on March 3, Poussaint *also* speculated, that the white devil must have made Taylor do it! He said that the shooter may be seen to have logically gained a "generalized hatred toward all whites" from his negative personal experiences. The Times reported: "He (Poussaint) wondered if the suspect had been 'abused' by a white authority figure, such as an employer or a police officer. 'Or was he stopped at some point for racial profiling,' he asked."

According to Ronald Hampton, executive director of the National Black Police Association in Washington, D.C., only the white devil can be racist (which is ridiculous). Questioned about the killings, Hampton told the Times, "It's impossible for blacks to enact racism on whites. Racism is the sum total of prejudice and power...and blacks don't have power in our society."

Tell that to Ronald Taylor's three dead (white) victims.

IN SEARCH OF OUTRAGE

What the case of Ronald Taylor and its coverage in the media reveals is a case of chickens coming home to roost. As I pointed out in "Hating Whitey," an entire academic industry devoted to promoting anti-white racism, housed at elite educational institutions like Princeton and Harvard, has flourished like a weed in recent decades. In this world view America is a racist universe in which black people can only be victims and only whites can be oppressors. It is an academic version

BLACK SPOKESPEOPLE

of the Johnnie Cochran school of racial prosecution and defense: indict America as racist, and let the culprit go free. "Anti white feelings...are not unusual " among some segments of the black population, Poussaint conceded to the Times. "Blacks who have such feelings against whites' may feel justified," Poussaint said, "because during slavery and segregation, a collection of whites kept them down."

Just imagine if white professors talked similarly about the racist who dragged James Byrd to his death. Eg.: "When asked about the lynching of Byrd, Dr. Poussaint of Harvard, acknowledged that it was a case of "extreme racism" but wondered whether the suspects had been previously 'abused' by a black authority figure, such as a boss or a police officer." What if this hypothetical professor noted that blacks commit nearly half of the violent crimes in the United States—many of which involving whites as victims—but speculated that whites who have feelings of hatred against blacks "may feel justified" in those feelings? A professor proclaiming views like these would be crucified as racist, and might even lose his job.

Fortunately, the three tragic deaths in Wilkinsburg have sparked at least one response from deep within the black left that gives cause for hope. If it is a harbinger of things to come, in fact, it shows one way that the troubled state of race relations in America might be turned around. In a column appearing in Salon, Earl Ofari Hutchinson has struck exactly the right note to restore moral balance in the black population.

Noting the "deafening silence by blacks" about this racial outrage, Hutchinson wrote, "Blacks must mourn these murders as passionately as they do those of black victims of white attacks, and just as passionately call for the harshest punishment of the killer(s)."

I chose to share an occasional article such as this to demonstrate my experiences with race relations, and my responses to the inequalities are by no means unique amongst whites. From everything I hear coming from today's black spokespeople I find it impossible to see them as capable leaders who can show us a way to achieve greater harmony. Shouldn't the leader of a segment of our American population encourage unification as Dr. Martin Luther King Jr. did, rather than separation?

A second article by Mr. Horowitz, from February of 2002, reinforces the notion that "drinking from the cup" is automatic for far too many of us. This article is entitled, "Racial Shakedowns":

An NFL coach has a mediocre season and is fired by the team. Jesse Jackson fires off a letter of protest. In Michigan, a 13 year-old murderer faces sentencing as an adult. Al Sharpton flies into the state and holds a press conference accusing racists in the criminal justice system of trying to take "our children." Hollywood launches a season where major black characters rarely make it to the screen in television shows on the big four networks. The NAACP threatens boycotts and two networks actually agree to racial quotas. The largest "civil rights" demonstration in nearly a decade is organized in South Carolina to protest the flying of a Confederate flag.

All these recent events have two features in common: From the perspective of the civil rights movement they claim as their predecessor, they are all laughable, petty charades; and their only shared purpose is to keep alive the idea that whites are evil, racist, and responsible for all the problems of African-Americans. The reality is quite different. The civil rights struggle culminated thirty years ago. What passes for civil rights activism these days is, as the above events show, no more than a political shakedown and a racial hustle.

FROM THE BOTTOM OF THE DECK

65% of the millionaires on the Green Bay Packers, the team that fired coach Ray Rhodes, are black. Rhodes presided over the first season in seven years that the Packers failed to make the playoffs. Furthermore, even Rhodes said he was embarrassed by Jackson's claim, supposedly on his behalf. Viewed along with Jackson's attempt to morph a gang of youngsters in Decatur who nearly caused a riot into civil rights heroes, this crusade makes both he and Sharpton seem like something of a public menace and, insofar as they actually are seen as role models, a true threat to black achievement.

BLACK SPOKESPEOPLE

Of course, Sharpton notwithstanding, the fact that homicide is still a major killer of young black males is deeply connected to the number of homicides committed by young black males. Treating youthful black murderers as adults is about taking black life seriously. It seems clear that Al Sharpton has no genuine interest in the problems facing urban black children, however. It seems that these black spokespeople have no genuine concern for any one in fact, except themselves.

Forget the arguments about the Confederate flag. The question is this: Is the flag a symbol of regnant racism? Are governments in those states whose flags incorporate the Stars and Bars into the design of their flags really bastions of Confederate diehards who want to keep blacks down? Elements of the Stars and Bars are incorporated into the flags that fly over many state capitals. Among them is Arkansas, which flew the dreaded symbol during the entire 12 years that Bill Clinton was governor. Yet he still enjoys 90% support among African-Americans, despite his willingness to fly the rebel symbol when he was governor. The flag means a lot less, evidently, than meets the eye. The holiday itself during which the rally against the Confederate flag was held—Dr.. Martin Luther King, Jr. Day—is the only day in the whole year that Americans set aside to honor the work of a single individual.

This is not about racism. It is about playing the race card.

A NEW KIND OF EXTORTION

Hollywood awarded the black actress Hattie McDaniel an Oscar in 1939. Twenty years ago, network TV created Roots, the most watched program in history--an eleven-hour epic that portrayed whites as evil and blacks as suffering saints. Throughout the 1940s, 1950s, and early '60s, Hollywood pioneered civil rights issues, and the cause of black America. Anyone who believes that liberal Hollywood is a hotbed of racism that practices systematic discrimination against blacks is insane.

Recently I was on Jesse Jackson's show Both Sides Now with ER director Eriq La Salle. The two black men complained that African-Americans are "locked out" of Hollywood, and only get demeaning roles. This is crazy! LaSalle plays a doctor on ER, a prominent role, and had just signed a three-year, multi-million dollar contract.

Yet, under threat from the NAACP, both NBC and ABC signed quota agreements for black hires because they were afraid of retaliation.

Now Jackson has set up a shakedown shop in Silicon Valley, home to what is probably the most racially diversified industry in America: information technology. Jackson is demanding that technology firms go out of their way to hire more African-Americans. If they fail to do so, they risk being branded racist.

Why is the media silent about this? The reason seems obvious to me: Democrats and other leftists run the media and the race card is the ace in the hole for these leftist politicians who need to retain 90% black support to hold on to their power. That is why Hillary Clinton has rushed to kiss the ring of Sharpton the anti-Semite, convicted liar and racist demagogue. In fact, the race card is so important to Democrats that Bradley and Al Gore have even begun to use it against each other.

Whatever people agree to say in public, no intelligent person actually believes the charge of racism holds sway anymore—but everyone is afraid to say so.

TELL IT LIKE IT IS

If the race card is power to Democratic politicians, it is both *money* and power to race hustlers like Jackson and Sharpton. Not long ago Jackson would go on tirades in inner city communities about "racist" liquor shops who were targeting the African-American population. As of this writing Budweiser is currently running commercials featuring black racial stereotypes. Ordinarily, this would be a Jackson two-fer. In the old days, Jackson attacked Anheuser-Busch for a lack of minority ownership among its distributors. But today, Jesse Jackson says nothing. Why you ask? Two of Jackson's sons were recently given the No. 1 Budweiser distributorship in Chicago, worth $33 million in annual revenues. And they got it, against all competitors, for almost no cash down.

Was the favor to Jackson's sons a form of protection money? You think?

While Horowitz's articles were written a few years ago, the fallacious accusations of racism that he describes are as strong as ever. Consider Hurricane Katrina, the recent Duke rape case, and pretty much whatever else happens to displease African-Americans at the moment.

Remember the riots in Los Angeles in 1992, stemming from the verdict in the Rodney King trial? Over a three-day period, large pockets of anarchy developed over 50 square miles of Los Angeles, essentially shutting down the nation's second-largest city. A dawn to dusk curfew was imposed. Looting was widespread as the poor suddenly saw a way to help "distribute the wealth." Over 1,000 buildings were set on fire, including most of the Korean businesses in the South-Central district. Dozens of people were killed, and thousands were injured and arrested before troops from the Army, Marines, and the California National Guard were able to restore order. Rodney King appeared on TV, asking his now famous question, "Can't we all just get along?" The riots were called the worst in US history—and most of the destruction was attributed to members of the black population.

I will never forget one moment in particular. In the middle of all the mayhem, Los Angeles Congresswoman Maxine Waters appeared on national TV with a background of burning buildings and looters running amok, making the statement that "Too many black men are in prison." What a jaw dropper! It was never more obvious that not enough black men are in prison. That goes for violent criminals of all races, men and women alike. How could Maxine Waters be so unaware that at the very moment she was making her statement, and in fact, at this very moment as you read these words, there are individuals (of all races, including blacks) all across the United States of America on the verge of or in the act of committing felonies that warrant prison time?

By making that statement in the midst of the flaunting

of laws and the general rule of order that the Los Angeles riots represented, the congresswoman seemed to be ignoring the criminality of those acts in her effort to be seen as a good black spokesperson. She was sending the message that, no matter what crime a black person might commit, black spokespeople would joyfully come to their defense. Compounding that problem, she continues to make statements like "No Justice, No Peace." If she's spreading this message of acceptance of criminal behavior, it's a safe bet that Maxine Waters is not promoting racial harmony or encouraging blacks to get along with whites. The Waters of *divide, separate, and group* run deep.

The examples I am bringing to light are not to diminish the legacy of civil rights activists. Certainly at one time in American history blacks needed strong and sometimes fierce representation to receive equal rights, civil rights, and integration. We are all fortunate that our country accomplished those goals through the work of great leaders like Dr. Martin Luther King Jr. But right now, at this point in time, it's overkill—and the fierce representation offered by contemporary black spokespeople is currently doing more harm than good. The way things are going I wouldn't be surprised to see Jesse Jackson standing in front of a black audience yelling, "Keep bitterness alive! Keep hate alive! Keep grudges alive!" Whether or not Jesse Jackson ever explicitly does that, the vitriolic and irrationality of his rhetoric leaves that sort of impression with too many people.

Jesse Jackson has done a lot of good for African-Americans by continuing the work of Dr. King. But he seems to have gone too far. Why do blacks even need spokespeople and so-called leaders in the 21st century? No other race in America has them, certainly not to that extent. Whites, Hispanics, Asians, etc. don't. Of course, if other races ever manage to get spokespeople like Jackson, things will only get worse.

On December 30, 2006, Jesse Jackson was at it again, speaking to a gathering of approximately 8,500 people, mostly black, at the James Brown Arena in Augusta, Georgia during memorial services for James Brown, the "Godfather of Soul" broadcast live on CNN and MSNBC. Jackson made the comment that "James Brown's music crossed over, but he didn't." What exactly was that supposed to mean? For one thing, James Brown had a white girlfriend/wife at the time of his death. Jackson also pointed out that Augusta was a slave port in 1862. Rather than attempting to reduce or eliminate racial anger, Jackson's subtle comments tend to reinforce it.

During the same time period, local black radio station WSOL V101.5 paid tribute to James Brown, devoting air time to his music. Almost every time I tuned in they were playing either "I'm Black and I'm Proud" or "Payback." There's nothing wrong with being black and proud, but I felt it was disrespectful to Brown to play those songs ad nauseam. James Brown publicly stated that he regretted recording the song "Payback" because of the negative racial attitude it created.

Blacks are being manipulated by the vast majority of these spokespeople who seem to see no value, certainly for themselves and their careers, in encouraging us to get along with one another. You can read divisiveness all over most spokespeople's choice of words. Even their constant use of the phrase "our community," meaning only blacks, has divisive overtones. In Jacksonville, when a black councilperson uses the phrase "our community," he or she isn't referring to the city as a whole or their council district's neighborhood, just blacks, who live all over Jacksonville, by the way. The same thing goes for the word "we" when spoken by many black spokespeople.

The way black spokespeople speak about the situation sustains and reinforces the embattled relationship between blacks and their "enemy": the white man and white supremacy. As evidenced by the irrationality of many of their claims, reinforcing this situation, nowadays, primarily benefits the spokespeople themselves, by making sure that they always have an impassioned audience. Fortunately there are blacks who have a voice in America who disagree with DSG and "us against them" ways of thinking. Three of these people are Dr. Bill Cosby, Larry Elder, and Juan Williams.

Juan Williams said in an interview that many African-American leaders have lost touch with a hallmark of the civil rights movement—the tradition of self-empowerment. Instead, they've embraced the notion of "victimhood."

"I think it's a terrible signal to our young people about who black people are to have us constantly wrapped in a cloak of victimhood, and to have black leadership that in a knee-jerk fashion defends negative, dysfunctional behavior."

Williams is the author of a book, published in 2006, called *Enough: The Phony Leaders, Dead-End Movements, and Culture of Failure that are Undermining Black America—and What We Can Do About It.*

Williams makes the point that critics often charge Bill Cosby, in his infamous speech at the *Brown v. Board* anniversary celebration, with beating up on an easy mark: poor black people. Williams says this is just wrong; Cosby's critics are the ones who veer off target. Cosby repeatedly aimed his fire at leaders in today's popular black culture who are often not just black artists, but the black executives who market and manage them. Cosby was also talking about current black political leaders and, most of all, about the civil rights leaders who, time and time again, send the wrong message to poor black people desperately in need of direction as they try to find their way in a society where being black and poor remains a unique burden to bear.

Cosby's point is that lost, poor black people have suffered most from not having strong leaders. His charge is that the current leaders—both cultural and political—misinform, mismanage, and mis-educate by refusing to articulate established truths about what it takes to get ahead: strong families, education, and hard work. Every American has reason to ask about the absence of strong black leadership. Where are the strong black leaders who will speak hard truth to those looking for direction? Where are the black leaders who will make it plain and say it loud? Who will tell young people that if they want to get a job they have to stay in school and spend more money on education than on disposable consumer goods? Where are the black leaders who are willing to stand tall and say that any black man who wants to be a success has to speak proper English? Isn't that obvious? It would be a bonus if someone dared to tell teenagers hungering for authentic black identity that dressing like a convict whose pants are sagging because the prison guards took away his belt is not the way to rise up and be a success.

Why have black leaders spent the last 20 or so years talking about reparations for slavery as if it were a realistic goal deserving of time and attention from black people? Why is rhetoric from our current core of civil rights leaders fixated on white racism instead of on the growing power of black Americans to determine their own destiny—power that is now at an astounding level, by any historical measure? Fifty years after *Brown v. Board of Education of Topeka, Kansas*, much of the power to address the problems facing black people is in black hands. Here is Cosby at the

very start of his famous speech: "I heard a prizefight manager say to his fellow, who was losing badly, 'David, listen
to me, it's not what he's doing to you. It's what you're not
doing."

Black Americans, including the poor, spend a lot of
time talking about the same self-defeating behaviors that
are holding back too many black people. This is no secret.
It's practically a joke. And black people are the first to
shake their heads at the scandals and antics of the current
crop of civil rights leaders who are busy with old school
appeals for handouts instead of making maximum use of
the power black people have in this generation to determine
their own success.

One of Cosby's sharpest darts thrown at the current civil rights leaders hit home a few months after his Constitu-
tion Hall speech. He was at a town hall meeting in Detroit
to speak directly to black Americans in one of the nation's
blackest cities. He wanted ordinary black people to hear
from him directly about his comments at the Brown anniversary gala. When he reflected on today's black civil
rights leaders, Cosby essentially asked why black leaders
were making the case for black crack addicts to get softer
sentences. Why are black leaders so concerned that cocaine
users get shorter sentences than crack smokers? Let's look
at the logic. It's true that the people snorting cocaine are
more often white and middle class, and crack addicts are
disproportionately black and lower class. You can make the
case for a racial disparity in sentencing. But what if all this
effort from black leaders was successful and crack addicts
got lower sentences?

"Hooray," Cosby said, spitting it out bitterly. "Anybody
see any sense in this? Systemic racism, they [black leaders]
call it." Then Cosby pointed out the obvious issue—but one
that the black civil rights leadership somehow missed or

underplayed. Black leaders, he declared, should tell poor black people to stop smoking crack. They should demonize anybody who does it. They ought to say that it is a betrayal of all the black people who fought to be free, independent, and in control of their own lives since the day the first slave ship landed. They should identify crack trade as one of the primary reasons why so many young black people are ending up in jail. Certainly, black leaders should be in front of marches, pushing crack dealers out of black neighborhoods. Their effort should include a message that has yet to be heard with sincerity from black leaders: using crack, heroin, or any other addictive drug, including excessive drinking of alcohol, is self-destructive, breaks up families, saps ambition, and is more dangerous than most white racists.

But I can't imagine that will happen any time soon. When was the last time you heard any civil rights leader raging against the clear evil of crack dealers, shaming them to stop selling crack? Has anyone seen those civil rights leaders at the head of a march against bad schools or leading a boycott against things like minstrel acts, sex, beer, and gangster images that are promoted as authentic black identity on Black Entertainment Television? *Essence*, a black woman's magazine, has taken the lead in condemning hateful verbal attacks on black women by black rap musicians. But the most visible black leadership is silent on these issues.

The good news about black leadership in America is that it has a history of inspirational success. Working against tremendous odds, black leaders have organized, built coalitions, trained, and inspired people of all colors to break through racism, taboos, and stereotypes to create the greatest social movement in American history—the 20th-century civil rights movement.

On February 8, 2007, television station WJCT presented *"ENOUGH" Is it Time? An Evening with NPR's Juan Williams*, which was taped for later broadcast. Mr. Williams is clearly a more experienced speaker and author than I am, but his overall message on race relations is very similar to mine.

After his 45-minute speech, and a 45-minute panel discussion, audience members were invited to ask questions. As it turned out, there were more comments than questions, and those comments were virtually the same as I have been hearing, especially from blacks, here in Jacksonville throughout the past few years in my efforts to improve race relations.

The first person up to the microphone was Jackie Brown, an African-American councilwoman and mayoral candidate who wasted no time calling Jacksonville a racist city, completely ignoring the excellent wisdom of Juan Williams. Ms. Brown stated emphatically that Dr. Martin Luther King Jr.'s dream is a nightmare. I happen to agree with her statement, but for completely different reasons. The biggest nightmare that I see is too many blacks like Jackie Brown using "divide, separate, and group" tactics, and indulging in the "us against them" mentality. Ms. Brown went on to bash the *Florida Times-Union* for their coverage of blacks and race relations (I don't see them as doing anything more than reporting the news). All of her comments were negative, but she still received a smattering of applause from the fairly well-balanced audience of blacks and whites. How anyone could expect to win a mayoral race while guzzling from the cup of bitterness and hate is anybody's guess.

Jackie Brown received 24% of the votes in that mayoral race, providing a good indicator of the racial divide that still exists in Jacksonville.

Sadly, Jackie Brown, community activist and previous

mayoral candidate, passed away Sunday afternoon, July 15, 2007. Relatives say she lost her battle with cancer. She was 43. No doubt Jackie Brown is heaven bound. Clearly, she had a big heart, and was passionate about her beliefs. Unfortunately, she served as a good example of what stunts the growth of African-Americans.

The next audience member to speak was a black man who called himself Bobby and stated that blacks should be afforded the same kind of psychological counseling that survivors of the September 11th terrorist attacks received. He commented that white slave owners took their women right in front of them, often impregnating them, and that black men literally whipped the babies out of them. He reasoned that the psychological trauma of these acts had been passed down over the generations and is responsible for today's angry black male. It sounds like questionable psychology to me, but Bobby's comment does make the point that keeping slavery in the forefront probably does more harm than good.

The last audience member to speak was a middle-aged Hispanic man who said he moved to Jacksonville in 1979, and race relations had greatly improved since that time, and Jacksonville is not a racist city.

It seemed almost bizarre to me, but some of the blacks who applauded Jackie Brown's negative and divisive comments still asked Juan Williams to sign their copies of his book. During his book signing segment I managed to spend a couple of minutes with Mr. Williams and mentioned that I had never heard a black spokesperson encourage blacks to get along with whites. He looked at me with a somewhat startled expression and said, "I thought it was implied." In other words, he felt it was obvious that blacks should try to get along better with whites. But as evidenced by the comments of the two black audience members, and almost all dialogue coming from the African-American population, it isn't so obvious. I believe that improving race relations by encouraging folks to get along is only taken for granted by whites. Blacks, especially spokespeople like the late Ms. Brown, seem entirely oblivious to the possibility that they could play a positive part in improving race relations.

Larry Elder is also among the precious few black voices in America that don't subscribe to the *divide, separate, and group* tactics or the "us against them" attitude.

In his review of the 2004 movie *Crash*, a movie about the allegedly tense race relations in Los Angeles, which won an Oscar for best picture, he asked, does this film square with reality?

The US Justice Department undertook a nationwide survey in 1998. They asked the following question: Are you satisfied with your local police? The results surprised local "civil rights leaders." In Los Angeles, the site of the movie *Crash*, 86 percent of all respondents said yes, they were satisfied with the police in their neighborhood. Eighty-nine percent of whites agreed, but what about blacks? Despite the 1992 riots, despite the horrific videotaped beating of Rodney King in 1991, a full 82 percent of black Angelinos approved of their local police in their own neighborhood.

William Bratton, a white man, runs the Los Angeles police department. But Los Angeles' first black police chief, Willie Williams, followed by up-from-the-ranks black Chief Bernard Parks, served as Bratton's immediate predecessor. Many blacks complain about racially motivated mistreatment or being pulled over for Driving While Black (DWB), but take a look at the numbers. The LAPD logs almost one million encounters with the public every year, from 9-1-1 calls to warnings for traffic stops. If casual in-

BLACK SPOKESPEOPLE

teractions are included, such as when the cop on the beat just stops to chat with a civilian, LAPD estimates the number of "encounters" would double or triple. Along with the total number of encounters, the LAPD also takes note of encounters that were problematic. In 2004, 4,907 public complaints were filed, of which, to date, 4,760 have been closed. Only 164 of the closed complaints were sustained. Of that fraction, 138 complaints are still pending a determination, but even if the full 164 complaints remain sustained, that's less than three percent of all the recorded interactions that police have with the public. The percentage would, of course, be much lower if all the casual interactions were counted.

Only 42 percent of the LAPD's sworn employees are white. Urban blacks know they are twice as likely to be victims of violence as whites. As a result, most blacks support their local police. Indeed, many urged the police to become more "proactive."

In Cincinnati, from 1995 to 2001, the police killed 15 black men. Of the shootings, seven happened after the suspect used a gun to either threaten, shoot, or resist arrest; three happened when officers were threatened with other instruments; one happened after a suspect attempted to run down officers with a car; and one officer was dragged 800 feet by a car and died. That leaves only three police shootings as arguably questionable, but in all three cases, the officers involved were acquitted or otherwise cleared of wrongdoing.

But in comes the then-President of the NAACP, Kweisi Mfume, who called Cincinnati "ground zero" for race relations. Mfume said, "Cincinnati's a microcosm, the belly of the whale. It's important for the nation to focus here on ground zero. If we can fix it here, we can fix it elsewhere. But if it doesn't get fixed here, it turns into anarchy, and all of us are left wondering, 'Is justice blind?'" As a result, the Cincinnati cops simply pulled back, became less proactive, more passive. This, after all, reduces the number of encounters with citizens, decreasing the likelihood that someone like Mfume could charge some cop with police brutality. The unintended consequence of Mfume's statement was that this troubled area of Cincinnati, known as Over-the-Rhine, saw a dramatic increase in crime within just a few months.

The criminal justice system is another target of black leaders' allegations of racism even though many studies debunk the idea of institutionalized "bias" against black criminal defendants. The US Justice Department released surveys tracking prosecution and sentencing by race and found that black defendants are prosecuted, convicted, and sentenced at rates either the same or (surprisingly) slightly less than white defendants with similar charges.

Remember Montgomery County Chief Charles Moose? He received fame for his work in helping to capture the Washington DC snipers. ABC News did a Person of the Week profile on him. It turns out that Moose intended to become a criminal defense attorney, but chose to become a cop first so that he could learn from the inside how cops planted evidence to falsely convict innocent defendants. "Because, as an African-American male in America in 1975," said Moose, "I really didn't like the police. I was pretty sure the police made up the things that they did so that they could be mean and—to African-Americans in particular." He decided to remain in law enforcement, however, when he discovered that cops rarely engaged in such illegal conduct. Larry Elder's review ended with... But, then, maybe he didn't see *Crash*.

Michael Richards, the actor who played the wacky neighbor Cosmo Kramer on "Seinfeld," triggered outrage with a November 17, 2006 rant against two black men after he was heckled during a standup comedy routine at the Laugh Factory nightclub in West Hollywood. A patron recorded the outburst with a video camera phone, and the footage spread rapidly over the Internet and other news media outlets.

Richards has made several apologies, including one on Jesse Jackson's syndicated radio program, in which he said he is not a racist and was just motivated by anger. Many observers, including an expert on body language, believe his apologies were sincere. Regardless, Jackson asked the public not to buy a DVD box set of the seventh season of the TV show "Seinfeld" that was released the week prior to Richards' outburst. Why would Jesse Jackson request a boycott of the DVD set? Michael Richards is hardly the only individual that would be affected by such a boycott.

In early December of 2006 the "Seinfeld" seventh season DVD was outselling the season six DVD (released on the same day the year before) by more than 75%, 90% over season five at some DVD retailers. An educated guess would indicate more whites than blacks would purchase a "Seinfeld" DVD. Even so, it's good to see a Jesse Jackson boycott attempt fail.

US Rep. Maxine Waters, D-California, charged that only situations such as Richards' incident turn mainstream media attention to issues involving the black community. "This is not simply about whether or not the black community forgives or forgets, this is about understanding that this is pervasive, that this happens in all our institutions, one way or the other," Waters said. As usual the congresswoman's statements went unquestioned and unchallenged. Nothing is more pervasive in our American society than the negative racial attitude of many blacks, which is encouraged by the likes of Waters. I have noticed a commonality between some black congresswomen like Maxine Waters, Corrine Brown, and Cynthia McKinney. It seems they seek the attention and praise of their constituents by automatically snapping up anything that displeases blacks and has anything to do with whites, and labeling it as racism.

When someone lets anger get the best of them, as Michael Richards did, they will say just about anything to cause hurt and pain, and more times than not it will be a shallow comment having something to do with the appearance of the person targeted, such as skin color (black, white, yellow, or brown) or weight or height or a visible flaw of some kind. I even heard one angry man call a barefooted man a "shoeless bastard." Both were of the same race.

One black spokesperson not as well-known as the "divide, separate, and group" pushers is Rev. Jesse Lee Peterson, described as the most courageous, outspoken critic of the civil rights establishment in America today. Often referred to as the "antidote to Jesse Jackson," Rev. Peterson is also the man behind a national boycott of the NAACP, believing the organization to be nothing more than a tool of the "elite, socialist" elements of the Democratic Party.

Rev. Peterson is the founder and president of the nationally recognized nonprofit organization BOND, the Brotherhood Organization of a New Destiny, whose purpose is "rebuilding the family by rebuilding the man." He is also the author of the bold and highly popular book, *SCAM; How the Black Leadership Exploits Black America*. Rev. Peterson is also a nationally syndicated radio host, TV host, and highly sought after speaker. Jesse is frequently seen on major TV networks such as Fox, CNN, and MSNBC, consistently leaving his liberal counterpart in knots. His unflappable, can-do attitude and absolute commitment to truth are the perfect medicine for our value-challenged society.

An exceptionally charismatic speaker, Rev. Peterson is a hit among audiences nationwide. Among his popular titles are "Rebuilding the Family by Rebuilding the Man," "From Rage To Responsibility," "Stop Reparations Now!" and "We Shall Overcome Civil Rights Leaders."

Character is the most important word in Rev. Peterson's vocabulary. Born on a plantation in Midway, Alabama, Rev. Peterson is this generation's Booker T. Washington. Jesse practices what he preaches, operating the BOND Home For Boys, a character-building after-school program, and many other programs and activities that benefit men and their families. His organization is a prototype for a bold new approach to solving our ever-increasing urban crisis.

From my perspective, the most visible black spokesperson over the last several years has been Al Sharpton. The first thing that comes to mind in regards to Rev. Sharpton is that he seems to be continuously accused of race baiting and various tactics that do more harm than good in addressing race relations. But regardless of the accusations, he always denies any wrongdoing. Something is wrong somewhere. Either he is constantly being blamed for things he didn't do or he is not completely truthful about his culpability.

One thing for certain I don't recall ever hearing is Al Sharpton encouraging blacks to get along with whites. Images of Reverend Sharpton seem to epitomize full-blown indulgence of "drinking from the cup." Not exactly what the good doctor ordered (referring to Dr. Martin Luther King Jr.).

I am fully aware that Rev. Al Sharpton has done a great deal of good for many members of the African-American population who think very highly of him, but from what I've observed, he's actually done worse than nothing to bring blacks and whites together—his rhetoric and attitude have helped push us further apart.

I'm very curious to know how Rev. Al Sharpton, and all other black spokespeople mentioned here see the "Promised Land," referred to in a speech given by Dr. Martin Luther King Jr. and how whites fit into it.

In November of 2006, an undercover policeman in a predominantly black area of New York shot and killed an unarmed 23-year-old black man and seriously injured two others, prompting Sharpton and other black leaders to hit the streets in protest, claiming the incident was racial. In days following the incident, some protesters carried signs that read "Don't call 911, the police will shoot you."

When Sharpton was asked why he was claiming this was a racial incident he said, paraphrasing, that he would stop claiming such incidents were racial when police start treating people in what he calls "our community" (i.e. mostly black-populated areas) the same as they do in other communities. Doesn't every born and raised American know that black populated areas are more volatile and violent than most non-black populated areas? I don't understand how in the world Sharpton and other black spokespeople expect police not to respond accordingly.

Of course there are some bad or rogue cops in police departments across America, and when those officers commit crimes while on or off duty, just like all other citizens, they should be brought to justice. It just seems as though Sharpton is always crying wolf, and that's not the quality one would hope to find in a leader. As the moral of the children's fable showed, sometimes there really is a wolf—and in many ways Sharpton seems to be the little boy and the dreaded wolf.

On at least one occasion, I can testify that I personally witnessed Sharpton letting black criminals off the hook. On August 26, 2000, Martin Luther King III and Al Sharpton joined to lead a march on Washington called "Redeem the Dream." The purpose of the march was to celebrate Dr. King's dream of racial equality, to commemorate his historic 1963 March on Washington, and to force action by the White House and Congress to penalize offenders of racial profiling and police brutality.

As I recall, the main focus of that march was on racial profiling. Early that morning I happened to catch Al Sharpton taking live phone calls on a CNN television show. One of the callers was a white taxicab driver who claimed that on several occasions he had been shot, robbed, stabbed, and beaten, and every time it was by a black male, which sounded like a pretty good reason for racial profiling. Al Sharpton's response was that he had been stabbed in the chest, an inch or so from his heart, by a white man and that didn't cause him to hate all white people. The taxicab driver never said he hated all blacks or any blacks. But he did give a good example of what the police have to deal with.

On the topic of racial profiling, that's something that will exist one way or another, either by police policy or by human nature. The term "racial profiling" originated within the police department. Whether it's explicit policy or not, anybody in a position of protecting and serving who repeatedly observes crimes committed by individuals of a similar appearance would be derelict of their responsibilities not to be aware of that trend.

In all fairness, since everyone has a race, racial profiling applies to everybody. For example, an elderly white woman in an expensive car, with a small dog sniffing the air from the passenger's side window, would likely fit the profile of someone more likely to be the victim of a crime than the perpetrator. When you stop to think about it, the black population, with guidance from black spokespeople, is massively racially profiling the white population with the pervasive attitudes of "divide, separate, and group" and "blame, shame, and complain."

Since the 1991 stabbing that Sharpton mentioned nearly cost him his life, Sharpton claims to have reevaluated his life and his tactics. "I gave in to being flippant, to shooting from the hip, to overplaying the theatrics and not the issues," he confessed. He has twice run for the US Senate since that stabbing, gathering 12 percent and 26 percent of the vote in his two runs, respectively. "Everybody grows," he says, adding, "I think we're not willing to give black leaders second chances because, in most cases, we're not willing to give them first chances."

He may be right about that, and perhaps for good reason. When it comes to race relations, African-Americans have two modes of operation. One is of self-celebration, i.e. Kwanzaa and the NAACP awards, which for the most part is African-Americans giving other African-Americans awards. There's the Dr. Martin Luther King Jr. holiday. We have the annual Dr. Martin Luther King Jr. breakfast in Jacksonville, which I have attended and have yet to hear blacks encouraging one another to get along with whites. There's the Juneteenth celebration, which I've attended and, again, found no mention of improving race relations. Juneteenth is the name for a holiday celebrating June 19, 1865, when Union soldiers arrived in Texas and spread the word that President Lincoln had delivered his Emancipation Proclamation. News traveled so slowly in those days that Texas did not hear of Lincoln's famous Proclamation, which he gave on January 1, 1863, until more than two years later. The proclamation declared, "That all persons held as slaves," within the rebellious states, "are, and henceforward shall be free." Thus, the Emancipation Proclamation was limited in many ways. It applied only to states that had seceded from the union, leaving slavery un-

touched in the loyal border states. It also expressly exempt-
ed parts of the Confederacy that had already come under
Northern control. Most important, the freedom it promised
was dependent upon Union military victory.

Although Juneteenth has been informally celebrated
every year since 1865, it wasn't until June 3, 1979, that
Texas became the first state to proclaim Emancipation Day
(Juneteenth) an official state holiday. But it is much more
than a holiday. Juneteenth has become a day for African-
Americans to celebrate their freedom, culture, and
achievements. Unfortunately, the event I attended was totally void of anything having to do with racial harmony.
There were, however, skits performed depicting dialogue
among slaves.

There are lots of other examples of blacks celebrating
black culture in organized ways. There is the annual Black
Expo, Black History Month, and Black Music Month; we
even have a Congressional Black Caucus Foundation, Inc.
There's the Black Entertainment Television network and
black beauty contests, just to mention a few. One thing that
seems to be consistently absent during Black History
Month is any acknowledgment whatsoever of whites who
have had a positive impact on the black population. A good
example of this is the civil rights act signed into law by
President Lyndon Johnson on July 2, 1964, which prohibit-
ed discrimination in public places, provided for the integration of schools and other public facilities, and made
employment discrimination illegal. This document was the
most sweeping civil rights legislation since Reconstruction.

The only other mode of African-Americans in our society is one of blame, shame, complain, protest march, riot,
boycott, litigate, and criticize white people, police, and the
government. Where's the balance, the middle ground?
There is none. Even with all that, we have many black

elected officials all across this country, and many are reelected. So Sharpton's claims of no first and second chances fit nicely into a category lacking fairness, understanding, and common sense, more commonly known in this book as DSG.

One aspect of "redeeming the dream" that everyone can agree with is eliminating police brutality. And as we all know, individuals of any race could end up on the short end of that stick. However, we must be careful to differentiate between brutality and controlling the uncontrollable. With fairness, understanding, and common sense being my own proposed guidelines for improving race relations between blacks and whites, I feel obliged to acknowledge that Al Sharpton seems to have softened some of his negative racial views over the last several years. Not a great deal, but nonetheless enough to notice. Could it be that he's come to believe whites aren't as bad as he would like people in his "community" to believe, and that if a change is going to come that makes America better for everyone, blacks must participate? Hopefully he will start speaking and thinking this way soon. For now, it's full throttle to "divide, Sharpton, and group."

Another black spokesperson who seems to promote racial divide is civil rights activists and NAACP Chairman Julian Bond, who in early 2006 delivered a blistering partisan speech at Fayetteville State University in North Carolina, equating the Republican Party with the Nazi Party and insultingly characterizing Secretary of State Condoleezza Rice and her predecessor Colin Powell as tokens. "The Republican Party would have the American flag and the swastika flying side by side," he charged. Calling President Bush a liar, Bond told the audience at the historically black institution that the current Bush Administration's lies are more serious than the lies of his predecessors, because

Clinton's lies didn't kill people. "We now find ourselves fighting old battles we thought we had already won," he said. "We have to fight discrimination, whenever it raises its ugly head."

He referred to former Attorney General John Ashcroft as "J. Edgar Ashcroft." He compared Bush's judicial nominees to the Taliban. The talk so infuriated at least one black family in attendance among the 900 in the auditorium that they got up and walked out in protest. "He went on and on name-calling," said Leon Delaine. "I walked out in the middle of his speech with my wife and three kids." Leon's expression of disgust for Bond's hatemongering gives me some hope, but although I wasn't there, I would be willing to bet that most of the other 895 in attendance cheered wildly at Bond's outrageous comments—a phenomenon I have often witnessed in person.

Of course, the harsh partisan rhetoric from Bond should not have surprised anyone who has followed him in recent years. In July 2001, Bond said, "[Bush] has selected nominees from the Taliban wing of American politics, appeased the wretched appetites of the extreme right wing, and chosen Cabinet officials whose devotion to the Confederacy is nearly canine in its uncritical affection." No racial Bonding going on here.

It's coincidental that Julian Bond would use the word canine, because for many years now I have equated much of Americans' negative black and white racial attitudes with a dog-like mentality. Have you ever seen a couple of dogs, usually male, who have never laid eyes on one another before, casually strolling along when they suddenly spot one another? They freeze in a tense position, hackles raised, and start snarling and growling at one another. From that point on, they could do anything from just going on about their business to getting into a fight to the death.

Amazingly some black and white American humans share that same dog-like viciousness. With his kind of rhetoric, Julian Bond should stay clear of dog catchers.

In his book *Enough*, Juan Williams makes the point that today's civil rights leadership is in older hands. Those like Jesse Jackson and Julian Bond are people who made a name for themselves in the 1960s, and are still fighting the battles of the 1960s. Latecomers such as Al Sharpton simply mimic the aging leaders. Neither the old-timers nor their pale imitators seem to recognize that national politics has changed and the black population they're speaking to has changed. Hell, white people, as well as Hispanics, Asians, and other immigrants, have changed. Yet the black leadership is fighting the same old battles and sending the same old signals even as poor black people continue to remain stuck in a rut, falling ever further behind in a global economy.

Juan Williams and the other positive cultural celebrities I mentioned are definitely on the right track. But overall, when it comes to dividing, separating, and grouping, or indulging in excessive racial team spirit, I'm not sure how blacks have progressed.

Chapter 8
ENJOYING HATE

What good comes from hate? Who wins when hate dominates? How can hate benefit humanity? Where does hate take us in the future?

Hate destroys, ruins, and kills, yet it flourishes among us. There are too many hate groups to keep up with, and I was extremely disappointed when I discovered that white Americans lead the pack in hate groups and hate crimes on topics ranging from race to religion, politics, sexual preferences, and who knows what else?

There are also black hate groups, one of which has had more coverage than the others by far: the "New Black Panther Party," which is not endorsed by members of the original Black Panther Party. The views, ideas, and teachings of Malik Zulu Shabazz, born Paris Lewis, one of the leaders and main spokespersons for the so-called New Black Panther Party, epitomize the main point this book is trying to make: that dividing, separating, and grouping on the basis of race is a nightmare for the American way of life. Shabazz seems to be brainwashed in his negative racial views.

One of the many goals set forth by the so-called New Black Panther Party in their Ten Point Plan is "freedom." "We want power to determine the destiny of our black and oppressed communities. We believe that black and oppressed people will not be free until we are able to determine our destinies in our own communities ourselves, by fully controlling all the institutions which exist in our communities."

The word "oppressed" is used throughout the Ten Point Plan. By definition, "to oppress" is "to dominate harshly: to subject a person or a people to a harsh or cruel form of domination." But since all Americans are, by definition, free people, oppression seems like an entirely moot point. Using extreme rhetoric often obscures the real issues at play. It does not help in the analysis and solution of problems.

The Ten Point Plan also states, "We believe that this racist government has robbed us and now we are demanding the overdue debt of forty acres and two mules. Forty acres and two mules were promised a hundred years ago as restitution for slave labor and mass murder of black people. We will accept the payment in currency, which will be distributed to our many communities. The American racist has taken part in the slaughter of our fifty million black people. Therefore, we feel this is a modest demand that we make."

I would like to know where it is documented that 40 acres and two mules were promised. It is my understanding that a Union Officer made that suggestion, but no agreement, formal or otherwise, was ever made. Also, it is impossible for me to believe that 50 million black people were slaughtered on American soil.

When Malik Shabazz gives an interview, he does nothing to mask his seething hatred for whites. One can't help but believe that individuals and groups that soak their souls in hate, consciously or subconsciously, actually enjoy it. Anyone who actively supports or participates in ideas of hate, regardless of their background or education, lives the destiny of a loser.

Too many black and white Americans have so little going for them that hating the opposite race gives them a sense of purpose, however pathetic it may be. Hatred is something that those individuals who possess it are allowing to control them. No one is forcing anyone to hate their fellow human beings, especially the millions of individuals they've never met and never will meet.

Generally speaking, a hate crime is a criminal act or attempted act against a person, institution, or property that is motivated in whole or in part by the offender's bias against a race, color, religion, gender, ethnic/national origin group, disability status, or sexual orientation group.

In the United States the most recent available hate crime statistics compiled by the FBI and published by the FBI's Uniform Crime Reporting (UCR) program are for the year 2003, and they indicate that there were 9,100 victims. Included are reports submitted by local, state, tribal, and federal law enforcement agencies throughout the nation. The report documents 7,489 bias-motivated incidents, which includes 8,715 separate offenses.

It's important to note that reporting by law enforcement is voluntary and it is widely believed that hate crimes are seriously underreported. During the early stages of the "Duke Rape Case" investigation, Malik Shabazz and the New Black Panther Party turned out in full regalia, intimidating local residents and chanting that the three white defendants be found guilty. When asked if they were armed, the response left little doubt that they were. Shabazz made a statement indicating that black women would no longer be mistreated by white men.

The white defendants and their families received death threats in the courtroom during the preliminary hearings. Jim Kouri, CPP, who is currently the fifth vice president of the National Association of Chiefs of Police and a staff writer for the new media alliance, wrote an article published December 29, 2006 titled, "Duke Rape Case Premise Based on Myth."

Kouri's article, in part, stated that this is a case that's ripe for the race demagogues who never miss an opportunity to exaggerate, spin, and divide for political reasons. This latest case of white on black violence is providing black activists, feminists, and liberals the ammunition they need to push their agenda forward: more legislated protections for blacks and for women, two major "victim groups" in American society. But the activists, politicians, and members of the press are working from a false premise, and crime statistics bear that out.

Dr. William Wilbanks, former professor of criminal justice at Florida International University, contends that the current perception of white on black violence, including rape and gang violence, is based on myths created by many with a political agenda. A top criminologist, Wilbanks has studied interracial crime for more than 25 years and he's been quoted by some of the top journalists in the business. When it comes to interracial rape and sexual assault, the statistics contained in the FBI's Uniform Crime Report and the Department of Justice's National Crime Survey during Wilbanks' study revealed that white rapists chose black victims 8,448 times.

However, black rapists chose white victims in 17,572 cases. In other words, according to Wilbanks, there were more than twice as many black on white rape cases as there were white on black cases. Overall white on black violence cases numbered 100,111, whereas black on white cases totaled 466,205. Therefore, blacks using violence against whites is over four times more likely than the reverse.

In New York, an incident occurred in 1988 that divided the city. A gang of white youths chased a black man onto a highway where he was struck and killed by an automobile. The prosecutors threw the book at the young men, who were convicted and sentenced for manslaughter. The crime became known as the Howard Beach Incident and the case became a book and a TV movie of the week. It was the case that pushed legislators to pass New York's hate crime law, as well.

On the other hand, earlier in 2006, a gang of black youths chased a white New York University student, screaming, "Get the white boy!" The student ran into a city street and was struck and killed by an automobile. First, the police denied it was a hate crime. Then, the prosecutors decided to try the case in Family Court, which means the worst these killers face is three years in a juvenile facility.

During the Howard Beach Incident, there were weeks and weeks of news stories, editorials, and opinion columns about the case. In the case of the NYU student, there was perhaps one day's worth of coverage. While the race baiters would have Americans believe that a growing number of blacks are victimized by white gangs in the United States, the opposite is true. The number of white on black gang attacks was 2,645, while the number of black on white gang attacks was 20,042. There were almost ten times as many black on white gang attacks as there were white on black attacks.

Interracial crime figures are even worse than they sound—and not for the reasons Rev. Al Sharpton and Rev. Jesse Jackson will tell you. Since there are more than six times as many whites as blacks in America, it means that any given black person is more likely to commit a crime against a white than vice versa.

Regardless of the findings in that article and many others like it, Malik Shabazz claims that even violent crimes by blacks on blacks should be blamed on whites. According to Shabazz, blacks never fought amongst themselves until Europeans came into their lives. Either blacks are playing catch up when it comes to violent crimes or Shabazz has been kicked in the head by one of those mules he so desperately wants.

Stephen Steinberg wrote an article in 2001 titled, "Race Relations: The Problem with the Wrong Name." According to Steinberg, the problem should be called "Race Oppression." His article, in part, read:

"Instead of public policies to attack structural racism, President Clinton provided us with the spectacle of a national conversation on race, predicated on the assumption that dialogue helps to dispel stereotypes, and is a tool for finding common ground. However, these bland assumptions are not politically innocent, as Adolph Reed argued in his column in *The Progressive* (December 1997)."

The problem isn't racial division or a need for healing. It is racial inequality and injustice. And the remedy isn't an elaborately choreographed pageantry of essentializing yackety-yak about group experience, cultural difference, pain, and the inevitable platitudes about understanding. Rather, we need a clear commitment by the federal government to preserve, buttress, and extend civil rights and to use the office of the presidency to indicate that commitment, forcefully and unambiguously. As the lesson of the past three decades in the South makes clear, this is the only effective way to change racist attitudes and beliefs.

Steinberg's article ended by asking what is it that we can hope for out of a presidential commission or the public at large, if sociologists, despite their assiduous labors, still do not see that good race relations are unattainable—indeed, inconceivable—unless there is a basic parity of condition between the black and white citizens of this nation?

One question that begs to be answered is, "At what time in American history has there ever been parity for the general population?" Basic parity between races cannot be forced into existence by the federal government in a society of free enterprise. To say the problem isn't racial division is at the very least absurd. What non-black financial entity with the necessary financial resources wants to invest in bitterness, hate, and grudges? Especially when the return on that investment is almost certain to be continued bitterness, hate, and grudges. At least for the time being, racial healing seems to be out of the question too. It's been my observation that racial wounds are not being nurtured to heal, they're being picked at to fester.

During Black History Month of 2007, a local theater presented a play that dealt with slavery. A local resident, in a comment to a local newspaper, noted that the audience was made up of almost entirely whites, which appeared to the writer as a good sign, because it showed blacks were not as obsessed with slavery as they have been in the past. A day or two later a black individual responded by saying that the reason for the racial makeup of that audience was because blacks can't bear to endure the pain of stories about slavery. That comment astounded me, since blacks treat slavery as a current event, and can't conduct a conversation about race relations without using slavery as a tool to promote white guilt. Isn't there enough individual and collective pain in present times to go around for everyone, without using history to give it a boost?

On the subject of slavery, I discovered some interesting

data. In 1860, according to the government census, there were 3,953,760 slaves and 488,070 free blacks, I never realized there were nearly 500,000 free blacks five years before slavery ended. In 1870, five years after slavery ended, the total American population was 38,558,371. The present-day African-American population is larger than the entire population of this country five years after slavery ended. So for such a large percentage of present-day blacks wanting 200 million or so whites to feel guilty or responsible for slavery seems way out of whack, seriously lacking fairness, understanding, or common sense. Not to mention that with such a large number of African-Americans in the US today, using the oft-mentioned term "our community" seems racially divisive.

One might wonder what an enslaved African-American from the 16th or 17th century might think about where their descendents are today. There are African-American billionaires, millionaires, presidential candidates, governors, mayors, congressmen, and black women district attorneys and judges. What would he or she think about the lyrics in rap music or the material in a black standup comic's routine? Or the freedom of hate groups like the New Black Panther Party? These are things worth thinking about.

Chapter 9
INTERVIEWS

In keeping with the purpose of this book, which is to share my own experiences, efforts, and observations of improving black and white race relations, I decided it was best not to conduct a series of interviews with other people. However, it also seemed appropriate to allow the mayor of this city and the head of the local chapter of the NAACP to express their views on the issue.

I mailed a letter to both Mayor John Peyton, and Isaiah Rumlin of the local chapter of the NAACP, informing them of this book and asking them to offer their views and opinions on how race relations might be improved.

I called the mayor's office about a week after I mailed his letter and was told by a member of his staff that because he receives so many requests for interviews, a committee has to decide which ones to grant.

About a week later I got a call from Reverend Rudolph Porter, an African-American who had recently been appointed to lead the Mayor's Office of Faith and Community

Based Partnerships for the City of Jacksonville. Rev. Porter explained to me that the mayor had requested that he conduct the interview with me. Naturally, I was puzzled. How could Rev. Porter, or anyone besides John Peyton for that matter, accurately express his feelings on such a serious issue? Not having much of a choice, I decided to interview Porter.

We met on the afternoon of February 28, 2007 at City Hall. Our meeting lasted only about 20 minutes, and Rev. Porter was very cordial and accommodating. When I told him that my primary question for the mayor was simply, "What do you think it will take to improve black and white American race relations?" the reverend said he didn't believe the mayor would want to go on record with an answer to that question. He also stated he himself wouldn't want to go on record answering that question. Doesn't that response speak volumes?

The reverend suggested that I send the mayor a second letter requesting him to answer the question himself. That letter was mailed about a week later and, unfortunately, has yet to be responded to.

I thanked Rev. Porter and got up to leave, and he walked me down the hall to the elevator. As we walked, he proceeded to tell me a story from his youth. When he was about six years old, his father would earn extra money on the weekends by washing and waxing his supervisor's cars. It was implied that the supervisor was a white man, though he didn't say this. On one particular weekend, when his father wasn't feeling well, Rudolph was given the job of washing and waxing the cars, but on that particular weekend it was raining and the task couldn't be completed. The supervisor told Rudolph he was going to pay him anyway and he could come back later to complete the job. Rudolph said he couldn't take the money until the service had been performed. He said the supervisor put his arm around him (the reverend put his arm around me to illustrate) and said, "I really like your father." Rudolph related this to his mother and said he didn't believe the supervisor liked his father. How could his father's boss mean what he said when he had two nice cars, and the Porters had none? Rudolph's mother told him she believed that the boss really did like his father. And from hearing the story, so do I.

As the elevator doors were opening Rev. Porter said he wasn't sure how to answer the question about improving race relations but he knew that economics were involved.

At that point my mind was racing. The elevator doors were opening, my parking meter had expired—and I had just heard the last thing I wanted to hear from a black man about improving race relations.

As everyone knows, you cannot quantify feelings. They don't fit very easily into a city budget or balance sheet. How can you put a price tag on relationships between millions and millions of people? What Rev. Porter's comment says to me is that blacks want financial restitution, and until that happens they can be expected to continue with the tactics of "divide, separate, and group," propagating an ongoing legacy of anger.

The reverend's story reminded me of one from my own youth. When I was in my mid-teens I worked briefly as a helper installing chain-link fences. On one rainy day, the owner of the fence company came out to the worksite and picked up a few of us in his luxurious Cadillac, even though we were wet and wearing muddy shoes, to take us back to the warehouse. On the way we stopped off briefly at his home, which had another beautiful car in the driveway, a swimming pool, and was on the waterfront. The thought crossed my mind, with all his wealth, couldn't he afford to pay me more than minimum wage? The answer is of course he could, but race had nothing to do with it.

I sent Isaiah Rumlin of the NAACP a similar letter requesting his input on the matter of improving race relations. This was not the first time I made an effort to contact Mr. Rumlin. Due to my frustration at the lack of positive participation from blacks during the JCCI study, I contacted Mr. Rumlin by phone shortly after that study ended in mid-2002.

Plans to write a book about my experiences were nothing more than a thought at that time since I had yet to attend the study circles, workshops, and task forces. Even so, I used writing about my experiences as the reason I called Mr. Rumlin. I'll never forget when I asked Mr. Rumlin if we could get together to talk about improving black and white race relations, and he immediately asked me what numbers or figures I could show him to support my point of view. When I told him I had no numbers or figures but just wanted to discuss improving race relations, he sounded a little surprised and said he would have to call me back.

After that we played a mostly one-sided game of phone tag for a few months. Rumlin only returned my call once, and unfortunately that particular time he got my voicemail. I responded but didn't hear back from him. As frustrating as that was, at least it was possible to reach Mr. Rumlin by phone. Mayor Peyton was entirely inaccessible to me.

Rumlin didn't respond to my letter until I phoned him about six weeks after sending it. Once we finally got the chance to speak, Mr. Rumlin was very personable and spoke in a friendly manner, much like Rev. Porter. Our conversation lasted maybe ten minutes, during which Rumlin officially became the third local black man with a strong voice in the community to tell me that he encourages blacks to get along with whites. Unfortunately, just like the other two, I have never heard or read Mr. Rumlin make a *public* statement along those lines.

When I asked, "What do you think it will take to improve black and white American race relations?" Rumlin essentially said that until the people in power put forth a concerted effort to conduct a true and honest dialogue concerning issues of employment, health care, and education, an attitude change is unlikely.

When I mentioned to him that blacks weren't the only ones dealing with those issues, and that many non-blacks, including whites, suffer from the same needs, he agreed. Since we were talking about "Race Relations," I asked him what members of the general white population might be expected to do to make a difference?

Whites are struggling with the ups and downs of everyday life, just like everyone else, although thankfully they don't carry the burden of being obsessed with their skin color, 24 hours a day, seven days a week. I explained to Mr. Rumlin that, other than my work in local efforts to improve race relations, which appeared to be going nowhere, and writing this book, I wasn't sure what else I could do.

At about that point he told me he was preparing for a trip to Tennessee and would call me back later that morning. I have not heard from him since.

I explained in my letters to both Mayor Peyton and Isaiah Rumlin that in fairness to my efforts I would include their response or lack thereof in my book. It had been my intention and expectation to meet with both of them personally and record their responses so their exact words could be transcribed. Since I never met with either one of them, I had to settle for what I got.

It's extremely clear that America's black leaders and spokespeople are putting a price tag on something completely intangible—their attitude.

Welcome to America's invisible (or not so invisible)

"Black Wall." For all the talk about reparations, it's silly to think that there's some exact monetary amount that could end the negative attitudes. It is also unfair for blacks to say, "We want the same things you want." Just wanting something doesn't make it happen, and by no means do all non-blacks have what they want. Blacks have positioned themselves to literally complain eternally.

In my second letter to Mayor Peyton I stated, "It may surprise you that I have an answer to that question of how to improve black and white race relations, and I would love to share it with you." That may be what scared him off.

As I see it, the solution to the question is very simple. Someone from the black population must come forward and encourage blacks to stop seeing whites as their enemy. Of course, that would be very difficult for any white mayor to do because it could make a bad situation worse. On the other hand, any mayor with the courage to take that stand, and the black individual or individuals who accepted the challenge, would make history in an almost biblical sense.

But as I've mentioned time and again, right now it seems that milking the suffering of ancestors is the direction of choice for black leaders and their followers.

HEYDAY PUBLISHING, Inc

P. O. Box 8925 • Jacksonville, FL 32239

January 24, 2007

The Honorable John Peyton
117 W. Duval St. #400
Jacksonville, FL 32202

Dear Mayor Peyton,

Hope this finds you well in all respects.

The reason for this communication is to reach out to you for help in my efforts to improve race relations between black and whites.

I am well into the process of writing a book about my efforts, experiences and observations of improving race relations.

F.Y.I. I was the only individual to attend every JCCI meeting on the "Improving Race Relations Study" in 2001 and 2002 which spanned nine months. Have also participated in the study circles, action forums, task forces etc.

A good deal of my book deals with race relations on the local level, however I am excluding anything to do with issues concerning the fire department simply because there has been no resolve.

It's my sincere opinion that you have done an excellent job on matters of race relations, a subject that affects the lives of us all.

I am requesting an interview at your convenience of 30 to 45 minutes for your input on this subject.

If you decide not to take part in this interview I will do my best to understand, but in fairness to my efforts I will include a copy of this letter in the text of my book including your response or lack thereof.

Please feel free to contact me anytime.

Sincerely,

Doug Saint Carter

HEYDAY PUBLISHING, Inc.

P. O. Box 8925 • Jacksonville, FL 32239

March 7, 2007

The Honorable John Peyton
117 W. Duval St. #400
Jacksonville, FL 32202

Dear Mayor Peyton,

This is a follow-up to a previous letter dated January 24, 2007 in which I requested an interview with you concerning my book about improving black and white American race relations.

On February 28th I met with Rev. Rudolph Porter, to whom you delegated that interview.

Although Rev. Porter was very accommodating we both agreed that only you could and should address this issue of such importance for yourself.

Rev. Porter chose not to answer what it would take to improve black and white race relations even on his own behalf. I wonder if that tells you anything?

Just so you'll know, I am only requesting two very brief interviews for this book, one from you, and one from Isaiah Rumlin of the NAACP. And so far, neither of you have shown much interest in contributing.

From my point of view this does not shed a positive light on our great city of Jacksonville, Florida when it comes to black and white race relations.

All I plan to ask you and Mr. Rumlin is, "What do you think it will take to improve black and white American race relations?"

Amazingly this seems to be a difficult question because no matter what the answer is it won't please everyone.

It may surprise you that I have an answer to that question, and would love to share it with you.

Mayor Peyton, even if you choose not to answer that one question for my book it could be very beneficial for you to allow me 30 minutes of your time.

As mentioned in the previous letter, what ever does or does not transpire will be included in my book.

Please feel free to contact me any time.

Sincerely,

Doug Saint Carter

HEYDAY PUBLISHING, Inc.

P. O. Box 8925 • Jacksonville, FL 32239

January 24, 2007

Isaiah Rumlin
NAACP
5600 New Kings Rd.
Jacksonville, FL 32209

Dear Isaiah,

Hope this finds you well in all respects.

As mentioned in our previous discussions I would still like very much to interview you for my book on race relations.

Quite frankly, I don't know exactly what I'll ask you other than your opinion on how black and white relations might be improved locally and beyond in the present and future.

It will not take an excessive amount of your time, perhaps 30 to 45 minutes.

It's my intention to be as fair as possible in this endeavor, that's why I would like your input.

If you decide not to take part in this interview please let me know and I'll do my best to understand, but in fairness to my efforts I will include a copy of this letter in the text of my book, including your response or lack thereof.

Please feel free to contact me any time.

Sincerely,

Doug Saint Carter

Chapter 10
THE BIG HURT

The emotional aspect of race relations is at the core of what needs to be changed in today's America. Too many African-Americans are locked into the thought that some sort of payment is the only answer to warrant a change of attitude. That likelihood is very unrealistic. One reason is, for too many blacks, no form of payment would ever be enough. Aside from wanting to benefit monetarily for something that ended in the 1860s, blacks also want whites to pay through feelings of guilt.

Requesting an apology for slavery is still on the slate for many blacks. The big question here is who should do the apologizing? Shouldn't an apology come from someone who is actually responsible for committing the act in question? Myself and millions of other white Americans feel very sorry for what took place in the slave era, but what good is an apology from those completely uninvolved and not responsible, given to those who are not victims of the act?

It's very clear to me why a high-ranking politician or

THE BIG HURT

American dignitary would choose not to give an apology to millions of African-Americans. For one thing, apologizing for something of this nature, considering the time lapse, lacks common sense. But more importantly, knowing the agenda of so many black spokespeople like Al Sharpton, Jesse Jackson, Julian Bond, Harry Belafonte, etc., an apology would be an admission of guilt, which would undoubtedly result in some form of massive lawsuit demanding restitution or reparations. Even so, regardless of the risks involved, apologies are taking place.

It's nothing short of amazing how blacks continue to dwell on so much negative history. Recently I read where Bill Cosby wants all Americans to contribute eight dollars each to fund a national slavery museum. The problem with that is too many blacks use something like a slavery museum for the wrong reasons, like hanging on to hurt and pain suffered by someone other than themselves and passing it on to coming generations, and justifying needless anger, bitterness, and hate.

I have heard some blacks say that we must remember the past so it doesn't happen again. It's unbelievable that intelligent, modern-day blacks could have that train of thought. There is no way on God's green earth that a return to slavery in America, or even a reversal of civil rights, could ever possibly happen. So rational reasoning or just plain common sense doesn't come into play for racial growth and maturity on the part of many African-Americans.

It's just my personal thought that Bill Cosby suggested everyone contribute to a slavery museum to appease so many blacks who were offended and hurt by his criticism of the problems facing a substantial portion of the black population, such as unwed teen pregnancy, high school dropouts, youthful disrespect, drugs, violence, and a propensity to blame someone else for their problems. It's really a shame that Mr. Cosby caught so much flak from blacks in his attempt to direct attention at problems that they need to address. What's worse is that some of those complaining were upset more by the fact that whites were privy to Cosby's comments than their validity. It's difficult to comprehend that blacks could possibly believe that the white population is unaware of the lack of control blacks have over so many of their children.

Listening to what blacks have to say in the various meetings and forums, it's quite clear there is a belief of a massive conspiracy against African-Americans by the white population. It's this kind of thinking that is so destructive to race relations. I can truly say that, although I am aware of white hate groups, never once in my life have I ever been approached by anyone or know of anyone who has been approached by any individual, group, or organization that has asked me, or anyone else, to conspire against a black individual or the black population in general.

Most of the pain blacks cling to is based on the distant past. It is history and the last word in history is story, so all of the tears, the anger, and the pain are what blacks are allowing to control their thoughts and actions. Too many of us, either consciously or subconsciously, enjoy not getting along with one another.

As of May 2007, Alabama became the fourth state to pass a slavery apology, following votes by the legislatures in Maryland, Virginia, and North Carolina. Alabama's Democratic-controlled legislature approved the resolution. Governor Bob Riley signed a resolution expressing "profound regret" for Alabama's role in slavery and apologizing for slavery's wrongs and lingering effects.

"Slavery was evil and is a part of American history," the Republican governor said. "I believe all Alabamians are proud of the tremendous progress we have made and continue to make."

On January 7, 2008, New Jersey became the first northern state and fifth overall to apologize for slavery, as legislators approved a resolution expressing "profound regret" for the state's role in the practice. The Assembly and Senate both voted overwhelmingly (29-2) to approve the resolution, which expressed the Legislature's opinion without requiring action by the governor.

On March 26, 2008, Florida became the sixth state to apologize for slavery. A solemn state Legislature apologized for Florida's long history of slavery, expressing "profound regret for the shameful chapter in this state's history."

Described as a bid for "reconciliation and healing," the House passed a resolution apologizing for state slavery laws dating back to 1822—decades before Florida even became a state that "perpetuated African slavery in one of its most brutal and dehumanizing forms." Earlier, the Senate passed the same resolution, with Governor Charlie Crist looking on.

Under normal circumstances, an apology does one of two things: it either falls on deaf ears or improves matters to some degree. Because the apologies of these six states deal with black and white American race relations and any possible improvement would depend on members of the black population, my experiences sadly lead me to believe that nothing good will come of it anytime soon.

While apologies are on the increase, more and more colleges are leading tours through the South—to cities such as Memphis, where Dr. Martin Luther King Jr. was shot in 1968; Little Rock, Arkansas; Atlanta, Georgia; Selma, Alabama, and Jackson, Mississippi—to help students understand the long, bitter struggle for equality. The trips bring events of that period to life and provide students with insights they could not get in the classroom, according to officials of Southern Methodist University, sponsor of one of the tours.

What percentage of black students taking one of these tours are likely to come away with the idea that we need to improve black and white race relations? An educated guess might be zero.

In discussion groups on race relations I always point out that improving race relations is a two-way street, and that a better understanding of the opposite race is necessary. And I always notice most people, including blacks, nodding in agreement. But it seems that blacks see whites as having the sole responsibility to understand them, not a shared responsibility.

Blacks should consider trying to understand the white population a little better. You'd never know it by listening to what African-Americans have to say about racial discrimination, but even before emancipation took place, most of the white population was never directly involved with slavery. Every president of the United States of America from George Washington to George W. Bush inherited slavery or its aftereffects. Try to comprehend the responsibility of freeing the slaves. There were approximately four million slaves. Most were physically strong, perhaps even stronger than the average non-slave at that time, uneducated, and very angry at the white population, even the white population that was totally removed and had nothing to do with slavery, much like today's African-Americans. There are even stories that some slaves planning large-scale escapes said that they were ready to kill every white man, woman, and child who got in their way. Taking the responsibility to free these people must have seemed overwhelming. In a perfect world whites would have gone out of their way to show compassion and help former slaves in every way possible, but there is no perfect world, and the white population had their fears and misunderstandings as anyone would. Of course there was much compassion and help on the part of whites, who should be better remembered for that. Let's not forget that once the slaves were freed, they were competing with whites for low-wage employment positions, which didn't make matters any better for race relations.

Listening to present-day blacks discussing American history, one is left with the impression that no one white should be credited with freeing the slaves, as though the slaves freed themselves. Furthermore blacks seem to take sole credit for all of their progress.

I get the distinct impression that blacks feel they are underappreciated by the white population. It's as if whites should throw them an annual parade to showcase their accomplishments. That may not be a bad idea, because blacks have contributed greatly in all aspects of our American society. However, it's difficult to celebrate someone when they are constantly growling at you. On the other hand, an argument could be made that blacks should throw a parade in appreciation for whites. Seen any slaves or slave owners lately? That sounds just as silly as the reverse. Either race-based celebration would enhance binary differences rather than encourage togetherness and a healthy relationship between all races. Maybe we should throw an annual black/white parade to celebrate each other.

The negative emotional aspect of race relations is alive and well. Syndicated columnist Thomas Sowell, reporting on the Duke rape case in May 2006, discussed racial polarization in one of his columns. He wrote that the worst thing said in the case involving rape charges against Duke University students was not said by either the prosecutor or the defense attorneys, or even by any of the accusers or the accused. It was said by a student at North Carolina Central University, a black institution attended by the stripper who made rape charges against Duke lacrosse players.

According to *Newsweek*, the young man at NCCU said he wanted to see the Duke students prosecuted, "whether it happened or not. It would be justice for things that happened in the past." Thankfully, the courts of this country do not seem to share this student's interpretation of the word *justice*.

But this student exemplifies the ugly attitude that is casting a cloud over the whole case. And the Duke case itself exemplifies the collective guilt and collective revenge attitude that has been poisoning race relations in this country for years. Racial polarization is a dangerous game, especially dangerous for minorities in the long run. We should look abroad for warnings, as this same sort of conflict has torn apart other countries around the world, from the Balkans to Sri Lanka to Rwanda. I don't think that there's any reason that the United States is exempt from such violent manifestations of racial polarization.

At one time, the black civil rights leadership aimed at putting an end to racism, and especially to perversion of the law to convict people because of their race, regardless of their guilt or innocence.

The young man at NCCU represents the culmination of the new racist trend promoted by current black "leaders" to make group entitlements paramount, including seeking group revenge rather than individual justice in courts of law. The same attitude poisoned the O.J. Simpson case.

Mr. Sowell makes some very good points. It's clear that the negative racial attitude on the part of blacks has not improved in the least bit since the O.J. Simpson trial in 1995 to the Duke rape case in 2006. A large portion of the general black population has a distorted view of justice. Whether a black individual is accused of committing a crime against a white, or is the victim of a crime in which a white person is a suspect, blacks automatically go into the "divide, separate, and group" mode, lending support based solely on race, while claiming to be concerned about justice.

Speaking of the Duke rape case, which never went to trial due to an enormous amount of exculpatory evidence, it's absolutely amazing all the support generated for the alleged victim on behalf of blacks. We've seen support for the alleged victim coming from Al Sharpton, Jesse Jackson, and the New Black Panther Party, among others.

Considering the fact that black women are rarely raped by white men, and that in about 15 percent of all rapes reported by white women, the perpetrators are black men, it seems like the black population's sense of justice is warped.

I've often wondered if 50 years from now will blacks look back on their conduct in these two trials with pride or embarrassment.

O.J. Simpson was back in the news in November of 2006 to promote a book and TV special entitled, *If I Did It, Here's How It Happened*. Thankfully, both the book and the TV special were eventually canceled due to public protest.

Fred and Kim Goldman, father and sister of murder victim Ron Goldman, fought for the book's rights because they wanted to prevent Simpson from gaining any additional profit from it. As a result of Simpson's August 2007 bankruptcy suit, a Florida court awarded the book's rights to the Goldmans to satisfy their unpaid $19 million civil judgment from 1997, which has risen, with interest, to over $38 million. Because the court ordered all assets to be monetized, the Goldmans say they were legally obligated to publish *If I Did It*.

A portion of the book's proceeds will be donated to the Ron Goldman foundation for justice, which works to support victim's rights.

The title of the book has been changed to *If I Did It: Confessions of a Killer*.

The Goldman family views this book as his (Simpson's) confession, and has worked hard to ensure that the public will read this book and learn the truth. This is the original manuscript approved by O.J. Simpson, with up to 14,000 words of key additional commentary.

During the week of Thanksgiving I caught Al Sharpton being interviewed on a cable TV show that discusses events in the news. The interviewer asked Sharpton if he thought O.J. was guilty of murdering Nicole Brown Simpson and Ron Goldman, to which Sharpton replied he didn't see enough evidence beyond a reasonable doubt to prove O.J. was guilty. In that same interview, Sharpton said something to the effect that his interests were in making America better. One would have to wonder how closely Al Sharpton followed that trial, which was carried live on Court TV and written about daily in newspapers all across the country, not to mention books and television documentaries, which came out following the conclusion of the trial and the fact that O.J. was found responsible for those murders in the civil trial in which defendants are required to speak for themselves. Members of the Los Angeles police department mentioned on numerous occasions that they almost never have that much evidence against a murder suspect. So how can Al Sharpton's comments on the trial be anything but race-based? And while we're at it, for whom is Al Sharpton making America better?

Sharpton often quotes the mantra "No Peace, No Jus-

tice." If his views of the O.J. Simpson trial are any indication, his sense of justice is not trustworthy. Civil rights
leader Andrew Young is quoted as saying, "Look at those
they call unfortunate, and at a closer view you'll find that
many of them are unwise." So goes many of Sharpton's
followers.

The wise might say, in reference to the reverend's followers, "No Brains, No Gains."

I have always felt that the nearly 80 percent of blacks
polled who felt that O.J. was innocent were making more of
a vote for skin color than forming an intelligent opinion
based on the details of the trial. It would be hard to find a
better example of "us against them," *divide, separate, and
group,* and "drinking from the cup."

It was never an intention of mine to dwell on the O.J.
Simpson trial, but it continues to linger on, thanks in large
part to O.J. himself. I happened to catch an interview on the
O'Reilly Factor with Michael Eric Dyson, a professor of
humanities at the University of Pennsylvania and author of
numerous books about race in America. He was discussing
the shooting of three black men by undercover police in
New York. I recognized the trend set by vitriolic and negative black spokespeople like Sharpton in Dyson's rapid-fire
speech pattern and one-sided view on race, so I did some
research on him. This man epitomizes what this book is all
about. If racism is a disease, and I believe it is, then Dyson
is a major carrier.

I found a 2005 interview with him about the O.J. Simpson trial, which was conducted by FRONTLINE on PBS.
Below are just a few of the questions he responded to.

In this interview Dyson explains the divergent ways in
which whites and blacks saw the Simpson trial, and argues
that it was the prosecution, not the defense, who played the
"race card." He also explores the possibility that the jury's

verdict was, in part, a form of "payback," and goes on to explain that the case was not just about O.J. but about generations of black men unfairly prosecuted by the justice system. "I think that what white America failed to realize with the quick jury deliberation, [was that] black people had been deliberating far longer than the O.J. Simpson case. So the quickness appeared in the case, but it took about 250 years to come up with that jury verdict."

Question: Was race the most important force at work in this case?

Answer: Well, when one thinks about the O.J. Simpson case, race is the most evident and observable and obvious difference. But there were many other differences tracing beneath: one, the level of celebrity in America—that if you're a celebrity, and you've got face recognition, and you've got high visibility, you're just simply going to get a different brand of justice than the average Joe Schmo.

Number two, I think issues of gender were extraordinarily important in this case; that is to say that women, who often don't receive a fair brand of justice in America, had hoped that with this O.J. Simpson case that the issue could come to the fore.

Unfortunately, I think many women who were white didn't understand the degree to which their black or brown or red or yellow sisters don't often receive the same kind of notoriety or infamy that Nicole Simpson did in order to get their cases heard and broadcast.

Number three, the issue of gender justice in America certainly is not high, and yet it did get some hearing in the O.J. Simpson case. We know that there are thousands, perhaps even hundreds of thousands of women, who daily toil under the brutal obsession of sexism or misogyny or other forms of sexual assault, whose cases are never heard, whose voices are never listened to and whose bodies are mangled and maimed, and yet we don't see them. So in that sense, there were many issues that were converging in the O.J. Simpson case. Race was the most evident face of it, but the body of consideration was much broader.

Question: What if it had been O.J.'s first wife, a black woman, who was murdered and not his second wife?
Answer: Well, when one thinks about the fact that O.J. had been

THE BIG HURT

married to a black woman—of course, his first wife, Marguerite, was a black woman—and allegedly Mr. Simpson engaged in some domestic violence with her, but the reality is that the body of a black woman doesn't rank as high on the totem pole of social consideration, as does a white woman.

Question: Even within the black community?

Answer: Well, certainly in the black community there's consideration for the black female.

On the other hand, there's tremendous gender injustice in black communities, where women's bodies just don't count as much as men's bodies. If Mike Tyson is accused of raping Desirée Washington, many black people rally around him. When Mike Tyson was accused of biting the ear of Evander Holyfield, it was seen as outrageous. So the ear of a black man counts more than the body of a black woman. That's in black communities as well, so I think that there's no question that the gender imbalance is very powerful here as well.

Question: But did the African-Americans rejoicing at O.J.'s acquittal really believe he was innocent?

Answer: Absolutely not. I don't think we should make the mistake of believing that black people who celebrated a) thought O.J. was innocent, or b) were even concerned most about O.J. as opposed to their Uncle Charlie or Bubba or their sister Shanaynay or their Aunt Jackie, who had been screwed by a system that never paid attention to them.

Again, O.J. was beyond his body. "O.J." was a term that represented every black person that got beat up by the criminal justice system, and now we have found some vindication, and guess what, white America? It was with a black man that you love. It was with a black man that you said was better than us. It was with a black man that you said wasn't like us. He was different than we are. He wasn't a troublemaker. He didn't cause racial consternation, or he wasn't controversial. Ha, ha, ha. The very guy you thought was so perfect turns out to be the one who turned the tables on you. That was a delicious irony of the victory as well.

Question: What about jury nullification? Was it possible that the jury knowingly set free a guilty man in order to send a message?
Answer: ...Well, if that's the case, let's just even grant the benefit

of the doubt that the term is legitimate and applies to the behavior of people, then my God, white juries have been practicing jury nullification forever. If that's the case, how do you account for the fact [of the] kangaroo court, where Emmett Till's murderers were attempted to be brought to justice, and everybody there knew they were guilty, and yet they were not convicted? That was jury nullification.

The history of white practices toward black people has been a history of jury nullification. So again, spare me the acrimony and outrage, because you've had that kind of acrimony and outrage for millions of black people who have been subjected to ridiculous levels of nullification by white juries for the history of this country.

Those are just a few of the questions and answers in the Dyson interview. What a guy. One can only imagine what the professor's students are coming away with.

I have found nothing in the words of Michael Eric Dyson that encourage the improvement of black and white race relations. If anyone has, please let me know. It's what I'm always searching for.

For one thing, Dyson makes the point that murdered women of other races don't receive the same notoriety that Nicole Simpson did. What other woman of any race has received that kind of notoriety for being murdered? Not many. On the other hand, when a black woman is murdered, it's usually by a black man, and if the media pays attention to it, then blacks complain that the coverage makes the rest of the black population look bad. So once again, blacks want it their way coming and going. Blacks often seem to prefer sweeping their trash under the carpet. I wonder if the professor ever makes that point in his classroom.

I'm also curious if Professor Dyson ever reminds his students that the slaves hated whites, and that many of their ancestors have never stopped? Civil rights leader Andrew Young is quoted as saying, "You have to expect that if you cuss the world it's going to cuss back."

THE BIG HURT

In the interview on the O'Reilly Factor, Dyson made the point that whites commit more crimes than blacks and that if the police spent more time in white neighborhoods, more whites would be arrested.

One thing that's for sure is that there are a lot more white people than black people, but Dyson failed to mention what sorts of crimes whites are getting away with. Ask anyone in the justice system and they'll tell you the police go to where they are called. Are we to believe Dyson would prefer police spend more time pursuing whites smoking marijuana in the privacy of their own homes, while blacks are committing rapes, robberies, and murders at a higher rate than any other race? If blacks cut way down on violent crimes, perhaps there would be more white-collar arrests.

I am aware that many students become fond of their professors and if that is true in this case please don't bother to contact me to defend Professor Dyson unless you can prove to me that he, on an ongoing and as widespread basis as possible, encourages blacks to get along with whites. From everything I've seen and heard from Professor Dyson, that's not very likely.

Chapter 11
HOW HELPFUL IS THE NEWS MEDIA?

With these words, I do not mean to encourage anger, especially the prevailing sort of needless anger coming mostly from the African-American population and promoted by the media. That is the last thing I mean for my efforts to accomplish. If the sum total of my efforts could be to help set the stage for improving race relations and encouraging racial harmony between blacks and whites, even if all I can do is get that proverbial ball rolling, I will leave this world a happy man.

One of the most consistent complaints I've heard in my community involvement is that there isn't enough good news reported by the local media. As always, news programs want to win the ratings race and live by the frequently used metaphor, "If it bleeds, it leads."

When is the last time you saw anyone on TV promoting racial harmony? Combine the fact that blacks show no interest in improving race relations and media folks who are ready in an instant to devour a negative racial story and what you get is a mess that feeds right into what the vast majority of black spokespeople are trying to accomplish, which is to "divide, separate, and group" while generating white guilt.

All the while they are asking for respect and appreciation, to live and be treated as individuals. Pushing and pulling at the same time negates any progress or growth.

It's so bad at this point that a white person of any notoriety can get in trouble even when they're trying to praise a black person. Terms like "articulate" and "clean" offend, as was the case with Senator Joseph Biden's compliments to African-American presidential candidate Barack Obama. Is it possible that if non-blacks weren't so accustomed to hearing the English language rearranged and altered by our African-American brothers and sisters it wouldn't be so noticeable? Most people would feel that those terms were clear compliments. Comedian Dennis Miller made a great point when he noted that the negative African-American attitude isn't so much about the color of skin, as it is about the thinness of skin.

Dividing, separating, and grouping along racial lines simply won't work. Do we buy a loaf of bread as a singular racial group? Do we apply for employment as a race? Do we pay taxes as a racial group? Even though we all may feel more comfortable around members of our own ethnicity, America is undeniably a land of and for the individual, and trying to change that would be a life's work wasted.

We all can and should support improving conditions of America's poor, regardless of skin color. However, many blacks, and especially black spokespeople, exacerbate the problem by making it a racial issue. If you are poor, you deserve whatever assistance is available; if you're not, you're on your own here in the 21st century. Getting on the government's dole based on skin color only prolongs the difficulties of becoming self-reliant. Poverty is an issue of class and should be treated as such in the best interest of all concerned.

Probably everyone's opinion about race has been influenced by someone else, a grandparent, parents, siblings, friends, neighbors, biased media stories, acquaintances—even teachers and professors can be a good or bad influence. My influence came from my father, who taught us that we are all the same on the inside and that a person's worth has nothing to do with the color of their skin.

No doubt, far too many of our youngsters are being taught the wrong message about their racial counterparts at home. It's been my experience that many blacks teach their youngsters, and try to convince themselves, not to trust whites. Trust, regardless of race or gender, is not the easiest thing to come by. Almost everyone, to some degree, is untrustworthy to someone, somewhere, at some time. So teaching your children not to trust the entire white race is not only ridiculous, it's dangerous.

Is there any race on earth that produces totally trustworthy offsprings? Most humans become untrustworthy as soon as they learn to speak. This all relates back to the core of most of society's problems, including race relations: parenting. And parenting among our African-American population has proven to be one of this country's most serious problems. Oddly, throughout my hands-on race relations experiences with all the blame, shame, complain dialogue from blacks, responsibility for the out-of-control segment of black youth was rarely addressed. And the implication was it's a problem whites should fix. It just goes to show how sad our race relations really are when blacks want to divide, separate, and group as a race, and at the same time want whites, whom they don't trust, to tackle a very serious problem that in many ways has gotten out of hand.

Regardless of what anyone wants to believe, the purpose of this literary effort is to improve black and white race relations in America. I have no political aspirations. I am not a politician trying to garner votes for myself or anyone else. I'm not trying to alter anyone's religious beliefs, and it's not about money. It's about a color-kind society. Kindness trumps the enemy, which is bitterness, hate, and grudges. There is absolutely no reason for blacks or whites to dislike or disrespect their entire opposite race.

Blacks and whites can definitely get along together and improve race relations; it just needs to be done "one at a time." Accepting one another individually rather than placing negative judgment on an entire race based upon the misdeeds of a small percentage of people, or holding an entire race responsible for the actions of their ancestors, is the fair and responsible approach to the problem. The white population seems to have made great progress in this area, with ample room for improvement. No doubt there will be blacks who claim they don't dislike or hate the entire white race, and hopefully that's true, but what I've learned, at least at this point, is that trying to improve race relations is like going up against a brick wall. It's that way in my hometown of Jacksonville, Florida, and seems to be widespread.

Speaking of Jacksonville, home of the NFL's fabulous Jacksonville Jaguars, *Black Enterprise* magazine revealed its most recent list of top ten cities for African-Americans as featured in its May 2007 issue. Jacksonville rounded out the list in the number ten spot. The top nine cities were: Washington, DC; Atlanta, GA; Raleigh-Durham, NC; Houston, TX; Nashville, TN; Dallas, TX; Charlotte, NC; Indianapolis, IN; and Columbus, OH. Surveys were evaluated and the editors weighed the following criteria as it pertained to African-Americans in each city: median household income, percentage of household earnings more than $100,000, percentage of businesses owned, percentage of college graduates, unemployment rates, home loan rejections, and home ownership rates.

Jacksonville had the highest home ownership rate of the bunch (49.6%), but it also had the highest mortgage rejection rate (30.2%). There were 6,799 black-owned businesses on the First Coast, whereas the national average per metropolitan area was 3,263. Downtown destinations like art galleries, museums, theaters, restaurants, and bars were mentioned as positive attributes for the area.

Nearly 25% of the population in Metro Jacksonville is black. Part of a *Florida Times-Union* article stated that improving race relations and economic opportunities for minorities have been goals for Jarik Conrad, chief administrative officer of the Jacksonville Regional Chamber of Commerce and the executive director of Blueprint for Prosperity. Conrad said the ranking provides hope that the community's efforts are paying off.

"It lets us know what the possibilities are," Conrad said. "We know what the challenges all are. But we also want to be the most culturally inclusive city in America."

A.D. Roberts, owner of First Capstone Mortgage Inc. and chairman of the First Coast African-American Chamber of Commerce, said, "We would be foolish to think it erases or negates any disparities that African-Americans face here, but anything that's going to attract black intelligentsia and African-American business concerns is a positive, not just for the African-American community, but for the whole of Jacksonville."

Having lived in Jacksonville, FL; Washington, DC; Atlanta, GA; and Houston, TX; I think that Jacksonville has the most room for improvement when it comes to race relations. Blacks seem content to let a negative racial past dictate the present and future relations with whites.

Since improving race relations is a goal for Jarik Conrad, I felt compelled to contact him to better understand his thoughts on the subject. We met and talked for about an hour and a half and agreed on several points of the discussion. The most surprising comment he made to me was "Why do blacks need leaders?" That's a question I've pondered for many years. I have no idea if he makes that statement during his speaking engagements. I doubt it, but if so, bravo.

Although I felt our conversation went well, once we parted and I took time to reflect on what had transpired, I began to realize that in a subtle and non-offensive manner, white guilt is a substantial portion of his speaking engagements, especially at the corporate level; it may be more accurately referred to as diversity.

Some faculty and staff members at a large southern state university have over the years been required to attend "sensitivity workshops" and undergo "diversity training." Typically, they said this training amounted to little more than being sternly lectured by a black spokesperson who told them for hours and hours how bad whites are and how much is "owed" to "people of color." Reaction from the staff and faculty was completely negative, especially since the lecturers didn't want to hear any feedback or questions. They only wanted to cram their own agenda down the listeners' throats. Attempting to close achievement gaps by using techniques of blaming, shaming, and complaining is becoming more and more obvious and less and less effective.

Before I became involved in race relations, terms like conservative or liberal meant very little to me, but now I see how divisive they are. The same is true when it comes to Democrats and Republicans, especially when dealing with issues of race. I registered to vote as an independent, not to vote for an independent candidate necessarily, but to avoid the stigma of either party. If this country was as great as it was intended to be, and as it should be, there would be no such thing as going after the "black vote." If anything, it encourages blacks to continue to divide, separate, and group. In the long run, maybe even the short run, that mentality is bound to backfire. This mind-set also affects the Hispanic and Latino populations.

If this country elects a black president, it's my belief that the general black population will ultimately be more disappointed than pleased, because that black president will be responsible for not only 300 million or so Americans, but also as leader of the free world, a great deal of foreign policy. And for that president to single out African-Americans for special treatment seems unlikely.

Chapter 12
TO KILL A MOCKING TREND

The fact that I was a radio personality for many years and toyed with stand-up comedy in the Atlanta, GA area in the early 90s should lend evidence to my claim that no one enjoys a good laugh more than I. And it's my observation that racial humor may put an audience at ease but in the long run leaves an underlying impression that our prejudicial feelings are okay.

When I first decided to try my hand at stand-up comedy, I enrolled in a comedy writing workshop to learn some of the tricks of the trade and the do's and don'ts. There was very little in the way of restrictions when it came to a comedian's material. The two main taboos, at least at that time, were using the "C" word, referring to a female body part, and insulting the African-American population if you were non-black, although it was acceptable to target a well-known black individual. On the other hand, the black comedians seemed to literally have no restrictions whatsoever and took full advantage of the opportunity—more evidence of black privilege.

If this book or one like it becomes a big seller and achieves national attention through the media, you can bet your bankroll that most, if not all, of the prevailing comics and comedians will feast on it for material. Late-night TV hosts such as Jay Leno, David Letterman, Conan O'Brien, and the majority of all black comedians will crank out setups and punch lines endlessly, leaving the impression that improving race relations between blacks and whites is nothing more than a joke. While this humor on the surface seems harmless and, for the most part, may be intended as harmless, it's far from it. A perfect example of this is the much referred to statement by Rodney King, "Can't we all just get along?" That comment has been mocked for the purpose of humor for well over a decade and a half now.

While Rodney King may not be the ideal individual to promote racial harmony, isn't that sentiment in keeping with the words of another man named King, Dr. Martin Luther King Jr.? As an individual who has always paid close attention to race relations, I've always wondered where Rodney King's statement came from. Was it something he said on his own, or was he prompted to make that statement by someone else, and if so, who was it and what race were they? So far, the answer to Rodney King's question is No, no thanks to present-day joke writers and those who perform them.

As far as minority comedians are concerned, especially blacks and Hispanics, it's extraordinarily rare, if it happens at all, that one gets through an entire set without a racial reference. Although this material usually gets big laughs, it tends to condone racial dividing, separating, and grouping. Granted, much of this material is funny, and we need to be able to laugh at ourselves, but this is one issue in our American society where encouragement for improvement is nonexistent and if you listen to some of those jokes they wouldn't be funny or even acceptable in any other setting. Of course, all of the material is exaggerated, and much of it is dated.

The fact that blacks rely on race so much in their acts reinforces the belief that that segment of the population is obsessed with their skin color, an obsession which is beneficial to no one in the long run. It's pretty clear that whites are afraid they'll actually have to do something to improve race relations with blacks when that's not true at all. An attitude adjustment is the answer and that doesn't even require lifting a finger, especially the middle one. Unfortunately, blacks still want to punish whites for something they didn't do, and for something that didn't actually happen to them. If that attitude wasn't so detrimental to our society it really would be funny

On April 4, 2007, the mocking trend received a major blow when radio personality Don Imus, in what was meant to be humorous, said the Rutgers female basketball team was a bunch of "nappy-headed ho's." Not only did that phrase originate from within the black population, by actual definition none of those words should be considered offensive. The definition of *nappy*, according to Webster's New Collegiate Dictionary, is *kinky*. How is that offensive? *Ho* is defined as *to attract attention to something specified*.

Admittedly, Imus' comments were, in reality, insult humor. No doubt, Imus picked up that phrase from a black man or maybe even a white man who picked it up from a black man, and probably thought it was funny and used it on the air.

Everyone across the board, from what I've heard, agrees it was a bad thing to say, and it caused a great deal of anger and hurt from both the standpoint of race and gender. Imus eventually apologized to his radio and TV audience, and also in person to the Rutgers basketball team and their coach, who ultimately forgave him. But thanks to heavy protesting on the part of Jesse Jackson and Al Sharpton, Imus was fired from his MSNBC radio show simulcast and, shortly thereafter, his CBS syndicated radio show. Bruce Gordon, former head of the NAACP and a director of CBS Corp., said he hoped the broadcasting company would "make the smart decision" by firing Imus.

"He's crossed the line, he's violated our community," Gordon said. "He needs to face the consequence of that violation."

There's that term again, "our community." Anyone who doesn't think that term is racially divisive just doesn't get it.

Don Imus returned to the airwaves December 3, 2007, on a different network with an addition to his staff of two black on-air personalities. They were immediately referred to as tokens by some blacks appearing on cable news programs.

During the furor that was expressed throughout the media in days following the comment, I picked up on a phrase I hadn't previously heard, the "race police," which was uttered by a black man, and no doubt is only out to nail whites. I say that because not only has the rap industry been guilty of much worse in regards to degrading black women or women in general, it does it endlessly. Where are the race police when it comes to all of the racial bias on the Tom Joyner morning show? Criticism of rap is nothing new. It began soon after the music emerged more than 30 years ago.

In 1993, the rapper-turned-actress Queen Latifah challenged rap's misogyny in her hit song "U.N.I.T.Y." That same year, C. Dolores Tucker, who was chairwoman of the National Political Congress of Black Women Inc., led an organized movement—which included congressional hearings—condemning sexist and violent rap.

In 2004, students at Spelman College, a black women's college in Atlanta, became upset over rapper Nelly's video for his song "Tip Drill," in which he cavorts with strippers and swipes a credit card between one woman's buttocks. In 2005, *Essence* magazine launched its "Take Back the Music" campaign. T. Denean Sharpley-Whiting, author of *Pimps Up, Ho's Down: Hip Hop's Hold on Young Black Women* and a professor at Vanderbilt University, said many black women resist rap music and hip-hop culture, but their efforts are largely ignored by mainstream media.

"It's only when we interface with a powerful white media personality like Imus that the issue is raised and the question turns to 'Why aren't you as vociferous in your critique of hip-hop?' We have been! You've been listening to the music but you haven't been listening to the protest from us."

Here's a thought: perhaps mainstream media isn't so vociferous in their critique of hip-hop music because blacks are offended anytime someone who is white criticizes anything that has to do with the black population, and they almost always call it racism. Hopefully someday, the accusing blacks will realize they can't have it both ways.

Something very good may come from all of this, and the unforgiving Reverends Al Sharpton and Jesse Jackson may find themselves on the hot seat. They may be forced to turn their energies on blacks guilty of the offensive lyrics in hip-hop music. Although they claim to be doing that and have been doing so for some time, it certainly hasn't been effective. It's my understanding that Al Sharpton is an occasional guest on radio shows that play the offensive music in question.

I can't recall ever hearing Jesse Jackson or Al Sharpton publicly going after a black individual or organization for any misdeeds they may have committed until the Imus incident. Sharpton called for an end to the offensive language that is commonplace in hip-hop music. It will be interesting to see if Sharpton is as vociferous or effective going after blacks as he is going after whites.

About a week and a half following Imus' comment, Al Sharpton said in a televised interview that he devoted a chapter in one of his books to condemning hip-hop language four years ago. What members of the hip-hop industry read Al Sharpton books? There's an enormous difference between addressing the problem in a book read mostly by those who agree with the writer, and hitting the streets of New York City with protest signs and appearing on major TV networks, calling for Don Imus to be fired. I haven't read that book, but I seriously doubt Sharpton recommended anyone be fired in it.

Jason Whitlock, an African-American writer for the *Kansas City Star*, made an excellent point when he said that blacks hold whites to a higher standard than they hold for themselves.

In part of a *Kansas City Star* commentary Whitlock said, "At this time, we [blacks] are our own worst enemies. We have allowed our youths to buy into a culture [hip-hop] that has been perverted, corrupted and overtaken by a prison culture. The music, attitude and behavior expressed in this culture is anti-black, anti-education, demeaning, self-destructive, pro-drug dealing and violent. Rather than confront this heinous enemy from within, we sit back and wait for someone like Imus to have a slip of the tongue and make the mistake of repeating the things we say about ourselves."

In my view, he didn't do anything outside the norm for shock jocks and comedians. He also offered an apology. That should've been the end of this whole affair. Instead, it's only the beginning. It's an opportunity for Stringer (Rutgers basketball coach), Jackson, and Sharpton to step on victim platforms and elevate themselves and their agenda$. Somehow, we're supposed to believe that the comments of a man with virtually no connection to the sports world ruined Rutgers' wonderful season. Had a broadcaster with credibility and a platform in the sports world uttered the words Imus did, I could understand the level of outrage. In the grand scheme, Don Imus is no threat to us in general, and no threat to black women in particular. If his words are so powerful and so destructive and must be rebuked so forcefully, then what should we do about the idiot rappers on BET, MTV, and every black-owned radio station in the country who use words much more powerful and much more destructive?

We all know where the real battleground is. We know that the gangsta rappers and their followers in the athletic world have far bigger platforms to negatively define us than some old white man with a bad radio show. There's no money and lots of danger in that battle, so Jesse and Al are going to sit it out.

In early May of 2007, I thought I might be witnessing a new and improved Al Sharpton. The reverend led a demonstration across Manhattan that saw him and a throng of supporters march to three of the four major record companies, calling for more "decency" in hip-hop lyrics. The rally came 12 years after a similar outreach was initiated by Time Warner music executives to develop standards for offense lyrics. At that time, however, Sharpton met with the executives and defended rappers' rights to use harsh language reflecting their impoverished upbringings.

"What do you expect them to sing, 'Hello, Dolly'?" Sharpton was quoted as telling *New York Daily News* in 1995. "I don't want to see Time Warner cave to criticisms from the right." Sharpton warned the company it would have him and other prominent black figures to deal with if it were to bow to pressure asserted by then-Republican Senator Bob Dole and others. The reverend has changed his tune post-Imus-gate and has since joined Oprah Winfrey and Russell Simmons in attempting to clamp down on rap music through various means. At first I thought Sharpton was expressing a newfound fairness, understanding, and common sense in condemning rap music's predominantly black artists for using the "N" word, *ho's*, and *bitch*.

Actually *ho's* isn't even a legitimate word, and the true definition of *bitch* has nothing to do with human beings. Nevertheless what Sharpton was doing in reality was condemning black rap artists for disrespecting a segment of the black population, especially black women. That's all well and good; after all, he is a reverend and should be involved in that cause. My question for Sharpton is at what point will he ever condemn a black individual for offending, robbing, raping, or murdering a white individual?

To date, as far as I'm aware, he always shows up to support blacks suspected of serious crimes against whites, or maintains a vigilance against whites accused of crimes against blacks regardless of the evidence.

He still reigns as the Reverend DSG.

One of the last things that Don Imus and Michael Richards should have done was make a beeline for Al Sharpton and/or Jesse Jackson. That's like catching a bad cold or the flu and treating it by spending the night in a meat locker. Your chances of improvement are nonexistent.

Chapter 13
NEVER ENDING STORY

As long as large numbers of the African-American population consider it hip to hop on the runaway blame, shame, complain train, improving black and white race relations will forever be in a stalemate. In July of 2007, the NFL's Atlanta Falcons quarterback Michael Vick came under scrutiny from law enforcement agencies for involvement in illegal dog fighting. Some of the charges against Mr. Vick included participation or knowledge of horrible cruelty, resulting in the deaths of many animals. Many blacks in the Atlanta area and other parts of the country immediately brought race into the issue, because Vick is an African-American. R.L. White, the president of the Atlanta chapter of the NAACP, urged the public not to rush to judgment regarding the charges against Michael Vick. He also referred to the media's coverage of Vick's case as a verbal lynching. Interestingly, I don't recall any NAACP chapter around the country urging the public not to rush to judgment in the Duke rape case, where the alleged victim was black and the suspect white.

On a nationally televised news program, two Michael Vick supporters, the Reverend Marcellus Harris and Minister Michael Mohammed, national youth minister of NOI (Nation of Islam) were asked, since the NAACP is coming in and making statements, is this a racial issue? Is there anything racial about this? Does the color of skin have anything to do with this? The Reverend Harris responded, "Well, we understand that race always matters (Michael Mohammed nodded his head in agreement) either overtly or subliminally. But we do not want to get into the race thing. We just want to see that justice is done."

On December 11, 2007, Michael Vick was sentenced to 23 years in federal prison, most likely a camp-style facility, with dormitories and jobs instead of barbed-wire fences and cells. The sentence means Vick will be in prison until at least mid-July 2009 even if he meets the federal standard of 54 days' reduction per year for good behavior.

Vick initially denied any knowledge about dog fighting on his property. He changed his story after the co-defendants pleaded guilty and detailed Vick's involvement.

The very fact that Reverend Harris would say that race always matters is clear-cut evidence that most blacks make everything a racial issue, disregarding the overall picture of fairness, understanding, and common sense. Every instance of misfortune that befalls African-Americans is not because of their race. Blacks are more likely to rush to pigment than any kind of judgment when it comes to justice. Too many blacks view their skin color as a disability and convince themselves it entitles them to some form of compensation. Ironically, blacks are mentally enslaving themselves in this manner of thinking.

A couple of African American professors decided to weigh in on the Michael Vick case, claming it was a matter of race. They were Marc Lamont Hill an assistant professor of urban education at Temple University, and the afore-mentioned Dr. Michael Eric Dyson. Professor Hill, appearing on at least two nationally broadcast TV news programs, said race was a factor because outside of the courthouse where Michael Vick was attending a hearing, whites were lined up on one side of the street and blacks on the other side. That is true, however, he failed to mention that the people lined up on the white, or non-black, side of the street were almost entirely members or supporters of People for the Ethical Treatment of Animals (PETA), while the people on the black side of the street were making it a racial issue, which was clear by some of the protest signs they were holding, including one which read, "Black Atlanta Loves Vick." So if Professor Hill was being the least bit fair he would have noted that only the blacks were making it a racial issue. He also stated that black athletes were treated less fairly than white athletes by the media in such high profile cases. I would like Professor Hill to name one high profile white professional baseball, football or basketball athlete that has been accused of, convicted of, or confessed to the murder of a human being or an animal. I can't think of one. With professors like this, blacks have a long way to go indeed.

Not to be outdone, Dr. Michael Eric Dyson, appearing on a nationally broadcast TV news program said whites treat dogs better that they treat blacks. I wonder how many dogs have received a 130 million dollar contract as did Michael Vick? For his reasoning Dyson stated that *Lassie* was on the air for 20 years, but singer Nat "King" Cole's show was canceled after six months. For the record, in 1956 Cole reached an agreement with NBC, who packaged *The Nat "King" Cole Show*. The first broadcast on November 5, 1956 aired without commercial sponsorship. NBC agreed to foot the bill for the program with the hope that advertisers would soon be attracted to the series. Cole felt confident a national sponsor would emerge, but his optimism was misplaced. Despite the musical excellence of the program, which featured orchestra leader Nelson Riddle, the show suffered from anemic Nielsen ratings. Nonetheless, NBC decided to experiment. The network revamped the show in the summer of 1957 by expanding it from 15 minutes to 30 minutes, and increasing the production budget. Cole's many friends and admirers in the music industry joined him in a determined effort to keep the series alive. Performers who could command enormous fees, including Ella Fitzgerald, Peggy Lee, Mel Torme, Pearl Bailey, Mahalia Jackson, Sammy Davis Jr., Tony Bennett and Harry Belafonte, appeared on *The Nat "King" Cole Show* for the minimum wage allowed by the union.

Even though ratings improved, still no sponsors were interested in a permanent relationship with the series. Some advertisers purchased airtime in particular markets. For instance, in San Francisco, Italian Swiss Colony wine was an underwriter. In New York, it was Rheingold beer; in Los Angeles, Gallo wine and Colgate toothpaste; and Coca-Cola in Houston.

Unfortunately, this arrangement was not as lucrative to the network as single national sponsorships. So when the Singer Sewing machine Co. wanted to underwrite an adult western called the Californians, NBC turned over the time slot held by *The Nat "King" Cole Show*. The network offered to move Cole's program to a less expensive and less desirable place in the schedule, Saturdays at 7 p.m., but Cole declined the downgrade. The show lasted for a total of 13 months, more than twice as long as Professor Dyson claimed, and was not canceled. Nat "King" Cole decided to quit. The show's demise was due to poor ratings and lack of sponsorships, not race where NBC was concerned.

The *Lassie* TV series received Emmys in 1955 and 1956 for Best Children's Series and also was the recipient of the Peabody Award for excellence in 1956.

Nat "King" Cole had dozens of hit records enjoyed by and purchased by blacks and whites. If there was an award for race baiting, Professor Dyson would be a top contender and no doubt proud to be one.

Fortunately not all African Americans with access to the media are as racially unfair as Professors Hill and Dyson. One example is award-winning columnist for the Kansas City Star, Jason Whitlock, whose view on Michael Vick's circumstance is much more reasonable. He has said, "We have to spell out reasonable and appropriate expectations for our young people and our athletes. We can no longer sit back, accept whatever behavior they offer up and blame racism when we don't like the results." Whitlock also said "I also hope our modern-day civil rights leaders stake out a consistent position on compassion. We can't demand it for Michael Vick and deny it to those we don't like, especially when it comes to high-profile figures such as Don Imus. Vick and Imus are both flawed individuals. They made gigantic mistakes from which they should be allowed to rebound."

R.L. White of the NAACP said "Michael Vick has received more negative press than if he had killed a human being." Whitlock says, "He's right, but Imus' defenders would probably say the same thing, and they would add that Imus didn't kill anything (human being or otherwise)."

Anytime anyone becomes a suspect in a high-profile crime, innocent until proven guilty seems to fall by the wayside in the media and public opinion, regardless of the individual's race. On Christmas Eve of 2002 an eight-month pregnant Laci Peterson of Modesto, California, was reported missing by her husband, Scott Peterson. Both were white, attractive, and middle-class. As soon as Scott Peterson became a suspect he was relentlessly hounded by the police, the media, and the public. On March 16, 2005, Peterson was sentenced to death and currently resides on death row in San Quentin State prison. Scott Peterson has not admitted any guilt. Had Scott Peterson been a black man, there's no doubt many African-Americans would have claimed race as the reason for his persecution.

According to a news story dated July 13, 2007, Senator and presidential hopeful Barack Obama assailed the Bush administration's record on race relations before an audience of 3,000 at the 98th annual NAACP convention in Detroit, Michigan, which drew applause and cheers from the attendees. Seemingly until that speech Obama appeared to have a balanced approach to black and white race relations. No one in America benefits when anyone panders to the NAACP. The NAACP, most black organizations, and the general black population dictate and control the state of American black and white race relations more than any president has for decades and decades.

Speaking of the NAACP, if the second "A" truly stands for advancement, shouldn't improving race relations be at the top of their list of issues to tackle? No doubt striving for racial harmony is not only *not* at the top of their list, it probably isn't even on the list. If they were as truly concerned about civil rights as they indicate, they should change their name to the NAAAP, which stands for the National Association for the Advancement of All People. Unfortunately most blacks consider diversity and inclusion someone else's responsibility.

Barack Obama has mentioned in many of his speeches that we need to eliminate the divisions in our society. He's right on target with that point, but way off target on who's to blame when it comes to race relations. The first black presidential candidate of the 21st century, Obama, has also stated that when it comes to improving race relations, economics is a major factor. However, he failed to state whether economics was just one thing on the list of things needed to be done to improve race relations or if it was at the top of the list or the only thing on the list. From my observations the latter seems to be the case.

It appears to be a fairly unanimous opinion now that our democratic presidential hopeful, along with the NAACP, all black spokespeople, black organizations, and the general black population have essentially turned their backs on the white population in the name of economics. In other words, blacks have put a price tag on their attitude toward whites. Of course, no one knows what that price tag is, or if it's met, what changes would occur from within the black population. It's absurd to think that the general white population has anything to do with the economic situation of black individuals. Most whites are struggling with their own economic situation.

Is it at all possible that the black population, having the lowest fourth grade reading level of all races in America, including Asians and Hispanics who don't speak the language, may have a bearing on future economic earnings? Could the high truancy level and the dropout level, and the high rate of teen pregnancy and single parenthood be an economic factor? Perhaps lowering the high crime rate and gang participation within the black population combined with excessive drug use and widespread bitterness, hate, and grudges toward the white population may have a positive effect on improving the aforementioned economics.

Obama derided President Bush's commutation of former White House aide Lewis "Scooter" Libby's prison term, noting black men routinely serve time behind bars.

"We know we have more work to do when Scooter

Libby gets no prison time and a twenty-one-year-old honor student who hadn't even committed a felony gets ten years in prison," Obama said.

Aides said Obama was referring to Genarlow Wilson, a Georgia man serving a ten-year prison sentence for having consensual oral sex with a 15-year-old girl when he was 17. A judge ordered Wilson to be freed last month (June 2007), but prosecutors were blocking the order. Scooter Libby was indicted on counts that included making false statements and perjury, while Genarlow Wilson was charged with a sex crime in Georgia where the president has no jurisdiction. So the comparison is unfair at best. Not to mention there have been several cases of late where black men have been accused of crimes much worse than Wilson's and set free due to legal technicalities. So once again, the real question is, "What are blacks contributing to improving race relations?"

During this same time period, NAACP leader Julian Bond compared the slow progress of rehabilitating damaged areas in New Orleans from Hurricane Katrina to that of lynching. Engineers working on that project categorically deny the pace of their efforts has anything to do with race and say blacks can say whatever they want.

The lack of "learning to love your white brothers and sisters" has now, and always has had a much greater degree of devastation on the American public than that of a Hurricane Katrina.

The name of that particular NAACP leader should be Julian Bondage, because bondage is how he prefers to keep the attitude of African-Americans when it comes to improving black and white race relations. It's nothing short of amazing that many black organizations across the country are campaigning to eliminate the "N" word, which usually is considered a derogatory term toward African-Americans and is mostly used these days by blacks referring to other blacks. And well-known members of the NAACP, Julian Bond, R.L. White (the R.L. should stand for Racially Lopsided), and others readily use the term "lynching" to describe topical issues in the news as a means of defending and encouraging the divide, separate, and group attitude of many African-Americans. The NAACP should now be an acronym for "Negative African-Americans Conning the Public."

Amina Lugman wrote an article in July of 2007 titled "Obama's Tightrope." For one thing, if the black population were not so determined to divide, separate, and group racially, there would be no such tightrope. Her article stated in part that there is no better example than Hillary Clinton's comment about the disproportionate effect HIV has on black communities. She said that if "HIV-AIDS were the leading cause of death of white women between the ages of 25 and 34, there would be an outraged outcry in this country. For Obama to have said the same words in the same fiery manner could have been political suicide. By forfeit, Clinton essentially becomes the black candidate; it's not a space America would allow Obama to fill."

There's no factual basis for Hillary Clinton's HIV comment, but much more importantly, she is taking advantage of the African-American population, because that's how they set themselves up.

The same such advantage was taken in the Duke rape case when a white prosecutor vigorously pursued rape charges by a black woman against three lacrosse players who were eventually exonerated. The prosecutor, Mike Nifong, took advantage of blacks' divide, separate, and group attitude for political reasons, which they fell for hook, line, and sinker by swooping down on the Duke University area like buzzards on fresh kill.

An excellent example of the "Never Ending Story" aspect of African-Americans promoting racial divide came in an August 2007 article researched and written by Casey Lartigue, Jr. and Eliot Morgan.

For nearly three decades, Memorandum 46, also known as "Black Africa and the US Black Movement," has been passed around by photocopy, word of mouth, and currently the Internet, making the rounds among talk-show hosts, politicians, and activists.

The Memorandum, as it has been disseminated, outlines a frightening government strategy, authored by President Jimmy Carter's national security adviser, to undermine black leaders in the United States and sow discord with Africans abroad.

The conspiracy outlined in the memo is an alluring but ultimately false story. On June 23, after a few weeks of research into the factual basis of conspiracy, Casey Lartigue and Eliot Morgan devoted an entire edition of their weekly political talk show to debunking it and other urban legends.

"Everywhere we looked, we found evidence that the document was fake," said Lartigue and Morgan in a *Washington Post* article later that summer. They cite many sources, including a 1980 news clipping in which the Carter administration denounced it as a forgery; a September 1980 National Security Council memo noting that the "scurrilous document" referred to nonexistent entities such as the "NSC Political Analysis Committee"; 1982 testimony by the deputy director of the CIA presenting Memorandum 46 as part of a dozen suspected forgeries by the Soviet Union; a 2002 article by Paul Lee, a consultant to the *Malcolm X* movie by Spike Lee, dismissing Memorandum 46 as a fraud; and the real Presidential Review Memorandum 46, a bland call for a bureaucratic review of US policy toward Central American issues. This last source, the memo itself, is readily available on the Jimmy Carter Library and Museum's Web site.

"We also contacted Zbigniew Brzezinski, the liberal lion who supposedly authored the memo. Not only did he say he had nothing to do with it, but the former national security adviser pointed out that in one of the versions circulating on the Internet, 'the idiot-forger could not even spell my name correctly.'"

The co-hosts of the popular show on an XM satellite radio channel aimed at black listeners thought that was the end of the story, but they were in for a surprise. They soon discovered the strength of legends such as the conspiratorial Memorandum 46.

"These are the airwaves in which the first president of the United States was a black man, in which AIDS was cooked up in a government laboratory to decimate the black population and in which major corporations lace their food with chemicals to make black men sterile."

On June 2, the two shared their exchange with Brzezinski about the memo on the air. A few days later, Lartigue was in the studio recording a promotional teaser for a second show that would explore the topic in more detail. The black production director was incredulous: "Are you telling me it's fake?"

They then sent the production director links to the Carter Library Web site, which were passed along to Joe Madison. Madison, XM's lead talk show host and a longtime activist, spread the idea that Memorandum 46 was genuine, but its power to capture people's imaginations far outweighs their concern for truth. After a show in May that explored the topic, he noted that he'd received 600 e-mails asking for copies of the document.

Over the next several days after receiving the links Lartigue and Morgan had sent him, Madison took to the airwaves to blast anyone who questioned the veracity of Memorandum 46. Morgan called in to Madison's show to ask him for proof. Madison's on-air response was that Morgan and Lartigue were engaging in counter-intelligence.

Armed with their research, Morgan and Lartigue returned to the issue on Saturday, June 23. The show addressed other urban legends, such as claims that the first US president was black and that fashion designers Liz Claiborne and Tommy Hilfiger didn't want black customers. In the final hour, they made the case that the anti-black Memorandum 46 never existed.

The following Monday, the station's program director berated Lartigue in a phone call, threatening to suspend the show or pull it off the air. "We agreed that we wouldn't 'attack' other hosts again, if that was to be the station's policy. The programming director made it clear that he suspected that every source we cited was part of the cover-up. The tense discussion grew into a heated argument, and the program director yanked the show off the air," said Morgan and Lartigue. "So ended our careers in talk radio. Looking back, we take our cue from Malcolm X, who said he wasn't afraid to just 'tell the truth.' We weren't afraid to tell the truth or to challenge sacred urban legends."

Americans have always loved conspiracy theories. We question official accounts about the assassinations of famous men such as John F. Kennedy and Abraham Lincoln, and wonder endlessly about the (alleged) deaths of Elvis Presley, Tupac Shakur, and Jimmy Hoffa. There have even been serious doubts about whether Neil Armstrong really walked on the moon. But according to Morgan and Lartigue, "Conspiracy theories take on a life of their own in the black population."

It can sometimes be difficult to sort truth from madness.

From the Scottsboro Boys to the Tuskegee syphilis study, our government has verifiably displayed a willingness to conspire against its citizens.

Likewise, keeping facts separate from emotions becomes difficult when theories are linked to hard data about real hardships. For example, black Americans constitute about 12 percent of the total US population but make up nearly half of the nation's AIDS diagnoses. That inequity, which is impossible to ignore, begs analysis and explanation. Laymen are always left to invent meaning for the cold facts of science, but don't always end up with logical conclusions. According to researchers Sheryl Thorburn Bird and Laura M. Bogart, more than 20 percent of black Americans think that HIV was created to restrict the black population.

A survey conducted in 1990 by the Southern Christian Leadership Conference found that fully one-third of black American churchgoers believed that AIDS was an active form of genocide. One-third also believed that the virus was produced in a germ-warfare lab. A full 40 percent of black college students in Washington, DC, agreed. An even higher percentage of blacks polled said they thought that crack cocaine was custom-made to be planted in African-American neighborhoods to keep them poor and crime-ridden. These beliefs and others make seeking the truth an uphill battle.

Syracuse University political scientist Michael Barkun writes in his book *A Culture of Conspiracy* that "a conspiracist worldview implies a universe governed by design rather than by randomness." In his analysis, three principles are found in almost all conspiracy theories: "Nothing happens by accident," "Nothing is as it seems," and "Everything is connected."

"We quickly learned there is a fourth factor: If you

question a conspiracy, you might be a part of it," said the ousted talk show hosts.

"Information is power." That was an early mantra of the black-owned, Lanham-based conglomerate Radio One, which runs XM's Channel 169, "The Power," which used to broadcast "The Casey Lartigue Show." Over the past two decades, Radio One has been a resource for black people who may not have the financial means or wherewithal to highlight an injustice.

"We were eager to reach that audience, and on April 21, 2007, we launched the show."

Casey Lartigue is a native of Missouri City, Texas, who spent time working for the advocacy group Fight for Children and as an analyst at the libertarian Cato. Eliot Morgan was raised on the South Side of Chicago, a former Trotskyite who currently studies environmental issues at Harvard. The stated goal of their show was to challenge orthodoxies of all types.

The show's theme song was Prince's "Controversy," and that's exactly what they sought to foster—and often succeeded. One of their guests, economist Walter E. Williams, irritated some listeners by denouncing reparations for slavery and dismissing the need for a minimum wage. On the 82nd anniversary of Malcolm X's birthday, the pair dared to ask, "What did Malcolm X do?"

"Judging from the response from callers, you would have thought we had confessed to assassinating the Nation of Islam leader."

Morgan and Lartigue say that they did get occasional warnings from others at the station, but dismissed them as meaningless office gossip. They were encouraged frequently by feedback from listeners who found the program refreshing.

"This was the provocative Wild West world of XM Radio, where shock jocks such as Opie and Anthony typically roam unchecked. No reason to be concerned, right?"

It is possible that the story of Memorandum 46 is just too good to let go of. In a world that has seen many smaller-scale conspiracies of governments against citizens, it is tempting to generalize the phenomenon. The memo represents just the thing that activists have been seeking to prove—that the US government was and is still plotting against black Americans in an organized manner. At the very least, it's a ready-made excuse for every disappointment or ill plaguing the black population. To the extent that the myth of the memo excuses blacks from personal responsibility, it is a dangerous lie that needed to be exposed.

There are many other examples of unfounded rumors stoked by blacks to support efforts of maintaining white guilt, with no end in sight.

Chapter 14
A LITTLE HELP FOR MY FRIENDS

Even before I became involved directly with the process, I've always hoped that I could be a help in improving black and white race relations. Amazingly, after years of seeking, I can't point to one individual, black or white, who publicly encourages us to get along with one another. I still see a white population that thinks for the most part that race relations are no longer a problem. They see African-Americans in all walks of life succeeding or failing, just like themselves and all other non-blacks. Most Caucasians are not immersed in the past. Instead they are focused on the present and the future. They are often unaware of the unrelenting negativity coming from within the black population, but when they see it they are often bewildered, disillusioned, and sometimes angered by it.

That's not to say there is no room for improvements on the part of white people. We all need to stop forming immediate negative opinions based on the very sight of someone from another race. We should keep in mind that even though we may never attain a truly color *blind* society, a color *kind* society is attainable.

Everyone should stop focusing on skin color altogether, and that's something blacks could work on quite a bit, too, since most blacks are so obsessed with their skin color 24 hours a day, seven days a week. Is it necessary for blacks to bring even more attention to their ethnicity by doing things like dressing in African-American clothing, and speaking in a manner not taught in our American educational system? There seems to be an inordinate number of African-American men with shaved heads. Are we to believe that this has nothing to do with a racial statement? Many African-American women have similar hairstyles. Over the past several years, I've noticed a great number of blacks wearing baseball caps with the New York Yankees emblem. There is no hard evidence that this is some kind of racial statement, but what else could it be? I've asked a couple of black men wearing such a cap if they were Yankees fans and they told me they were not, and gave no further explanation. Since American blacks seem to be trendsetters, it's no surprise that many non-blacks have picked up on some of these apparent social statements, probably unaware of their ultimate meanings. The big question is what good is accomplished by these and other divisive actions? I can only surmise that it must somehow help keep those egotistical, self-serving black spokespeople in the forefront who continue to ignore any attempt to encourage racial harmony.

I once heard someone pose the question that if African-Americans feel so hurt by the history of slavery, would they go back in time, if it were possible, and eliminate slavery entirely? This means that they would have been born and raised in Africa instead of here in America, and would most likely still be living there. I'm sure there are blacks big-hearted enough to do just that. If that's the case, why aren't they big hearted enough to stop holding present-day whites and the government responsible for something perpetrated by a small percentage of our American white ancestors—something present-day whites had nothing to do with?

Another bizarre aspect of race relations is how African-Americans have such a great, undying love for Dr. Martin Luther King, Jr. and Jesus Christ. Dr. King, as we all know, envisioned blacks and whites getting along with one another. Why else would he have said, "Learn to love your white brothers and sisters; don't drink from the cup of bitterness and hate"? As for Jesus Christ, who in their right mind could possibly comprehend he would condone drinking from that cup of bitterness and hate? The admiration felt for these two figures, contrasted with the overwhelming negativity of the majority of blacks toward whites, is a glaring example of their typical lack of fairness, understanding, and common sense, and is an example of how blacks actively do not want to get along with whites. If they do want to get along with whites, I've yet to see the proof. Where is the intelligence in such a negative attitude? How can not getting along with an entire race in America be a good thing?

It's puzzling to me how blacks can claim to love America so much and still dislike whites. It's like someone saying they love to swim, but don't like water.

Doesn't it seem fair to consider the majority of blacks in the USA are African-Americans in that order, Africans first, Americans further down the list? Wouldn't that help explain the dividing, separating, and grouping?

All of humanity is flawed, collectively and individually. Throughout my lifetime, I've uttered negative remarks of others and laughed at humor that many would find offensive. I've felt guilt for these things, but am also aware that I personally and my racial ethnicity have been the target of offensive comments and humor.

This literary effort is not about me; it's about perhaps the most important part of American race relations dialogue that never gets attention. It's about learning to appreciate, not depreciate, our opposite race.

The racial team spirit mentioned in my open letter to JCCI seems to be fairly normal. It's the "excessive" aspect that needs to be addressed to create a better America. The way we react to someone who appears different than ourselves could be human nature or a learned behavior or a combination thereof. Either way, we as individuals have the ability to control that behavior. This is one more example of how parenting is greatly responsible for how we relate to one another. Teaching racism or even insinuating someone should dislike, hate, or distrust an individual of another race, let alone the entire race, is un-American and unintelligent.

Due to the manmade complexities of race relations, I found it somewhat difficult to get this project started, and have found the conclusion of this book to be even more difficult. At some point, the writing had to end and the publishing processes begin, even though claims of racial injustice, both locally and nationally, continue to make news almost daily. Injustice is not exclusive to the black population, but claiming that every accusation of wrongdoing is based on race certainly seems to be.

In his book, *A Bound Man: Why We Are Excited About Obama and Why He Can't Win*, author Shelby Steele relates a great deal of interesting information about black and white American race relations. He discusses a phenomenon that I've been aware of for as long as I can remember, called "masking." As Steele describes it,

BLACK AMERICANS IN THE 21ST CENTURY

"We (blacks) have two narratives: what we tell each other and what we tell whites. When it comes to present-day race relations, he describes blacks as being either bargainers or challengers. When bargainers in any walk of life seek success in the American mainstream, they make a very specific deal with whites (individuals and institutions): 'I will not use America's horrible history of white racism against you, if you will promise not to use my race against me.'"

According to the author, in the 80s, the Bill Cosby show made the classic bargainer's deal with its vast white audience. Other bargainers include Oprah Winfrey and Barack Obama.

The challenger's code, on the other hand, states that whites are incorrigibly racist until they do something to prove otherwise. Al Sharpton is a challenger. Sharpton, according to the author, with little education or talent beyond being fast on his feet, relies entirely on the power of racial stigmatizing to make his way in America.

Challengers tell American institutions that they must practice affirmative action and diversity or have their legitimacy destroyed. And so institutions become obsessed with the idea of "diversity," not because affirmative action actually helps achieve anything, but because promoting oneself or one's organization as diverse fends off stigma, and fends off the challengers. The divide, separate, and group brigade referred to in this book would certainly fall under the category of challengers, and unfortunately, they far outnumber the bargainers.

Bargainers and challengers, as psychological types, are certainly found in many areas of life besides race. But when it comes to race relations, I would have to put myself in the rare classification of being a challenging bargainer. I challenge blacks to put forth an effort to improve race relations with whites without including a price tag, and at the same time I promise to continue to respect all individuals equally; to promote fairness, understanding, and common sense for the betterment of everyone, and to pray that respect is returned in kind.

This book will go to print and publication before the November 2008 presidential election is held; however, at this time, Barack Obama, who is black, is not only a viable candidate, he appears to have a very good chance of going all the way. And as far as race relations are concerned, one thing can be etched in stone. Regardless of the outcome, win or lose, it will be a racial issue where American blacks are concerned. At least at this point, Barack Obama does not look like a bound man in any way, shape, or form.

From my observation, Barack Obama is the only black American individual who is not an athlete or entertainer who gets a great deal of media exposure and doesn't make almost everything he speaks about a racial issue. One can only pray that if he is elected into office, that will continue. Anyone with great intelligence and wisdom knows every grievance blacks may have is not about race. Hopefully, America's black spokespeople can learn from this.

In the *Florida Times-Union's* February 11, 2008 edition, African-American columnist Tonyaa Weathersbee's editorial titled "Black support for Obama is partly a matter of pride," stated in part, "After all the Super Tuesday confetti had settled, I half expected for this sort of silliness to come spilling out."

It goes something like this: The black voters who overwhelmingly put Democratic presidential candidate Barack Obama over the top in key states like Illinois, Georgia, and South Carolina are racists who care more about skin color than qualifications. Already, one right wing pundit has likened black support of Obama to black support of O.J. Simpson; blacks see his rise as payback time. That's dumb, of course. But it isn't surprising. When it comes to Obama, black folks can't catch a break.

First we get accused of being caught up in our own stereotypes by questioning whether Obama, with his biracial heritage and his lack of civil rights pedigree, is black enough. Then, when Obama appears to be convincing a lot of white Americans—including huge numbers of white male Democratic voters—that he has the stuff to be president, the blacks who toss their support behind him get accused of seeing only race, when, in reality, they probably see the same thing the white voters who support him see: change and hope.

It would be disingenuous of me to say that race isn't playing a role in black support of Obama. I'm sure that for many black voters, it probably is. After more than 200 years of being treated as inferior, of being conditioned to believe that the only way to get the rest of America to see you is by singing or dancing or making others laugh, it should be understandable that black people would be proud of a black man like Obama, who is gaining people's trust without having to do that. That's about pride; nothing more, nothing less.

Ms. Weathersbee went on to say, among other things, "Obama's candidacy generates hope about inclusion, not dreams of payback."

I can only wonder who Ms Weathersbee thinks she's kidding. When it comes to blacks, everything, regardless of pride, is about race. Even in 2008, most blacks still claim they believe O.J. Simpson to be not guilty for the murders of which he was accused. That's all about race.

Hurricane Katrina is a racial issue even though it affected many non-blacks; the Duke "non-rape case" was all about race; the Michael Vick dog-fighting case was all about race among a large segment of the black population, including NAACP spokespeople, just to mention a few.

And we're supposed to believe Ms. Weathersbee when she says that a massive black voter turnout for an African-American presidential candidate is not mostly about skin color? Please.

From all I've heard, those accusations she mentioned are coming mostly from present-day black spokespeople, who are almost entirely racial challengers and supporters of the divide, separate, and group attitude, of which I would include Ms. Weathersbee. They're afraid that the fires of blame, shame, and complain may soon be doused by an intelligent, fair-minded black man. However, skin color may override even that sentiment.

In a February 2008 *Wall Street Journal* opinion column, Daniel Henninger writes, "There is nothing complicated about his (Obama's) appeal to black voters. Why should there be? And the mist of 'change' aside, are many whites, as some suggest, supporting him as a once-and-for all exorcism of guilt? Maybe, but I think it has more to do with frustration across the political spectrum over the urban black status quo."

The prism through which I'd like to view Obama's appeal is Bill Cosby. Cosby's TV show about the Huxtable family, from 1984 to 1992, wasn't just a sitcom. His "post-racial" middle-class Huxtables were an explicit attempt by him to stanch the downward pitch of black street culture. He lost.

In his current book, *Come On, People*, written with psychiatrist Alvin Poussaint, Cosby lists the grim, by-now familiar data on the social pathologies of black males. As before, he hammers popular black culture:

"The Ku Klux Klan could not have devised a media culture as destructive." The famous Million Man March of 1995, Cosby says, didn't make a dent. "What do record producers think when they churn out that gangsta rap with anti-social, women-hating messages?" He said, "Martin and Malcolm and Medgar Evers must be turning over in their graves." For many, the pull and potency of this media-led downward mobility made it seem an impossible situation. The book is a self-help road map to going in another direction. Henninger concludes his article by saying, "Barack Obama may be taking his country to a new place on racial politics. His party's politics looks like a higher mountain."

We should all be proud of the campaign Barack Obama is running. Without a great deal of support from white voters, there would be no chance for a black individual to become president of the United States of America.

During the last mayoral race here in Jacksonville, Florida, where Ms. Weathersbee and I reside, one of the candidates was an African-American woman who ran a very racially negative campaign and received 24% of the vote, mostly from black supporters. Yet in the 2008 Florida presidential primary, Hillary Clinton won the state, but Barack Obama won Duval County, which is primarily Jacksonville. What we are seeing is clear-cut evidence that the white population is showing a great deal of maturity when it comes to black and white race relations. But where's the acknowledgment for that? And where is the racial maturity on the part of the black population?

If the African-American population is so victimized, oppressed, and discriminated against, how could a black presidential candidate get even this far? It's not possible. One of the biggest questions lingering in my mind is if Barack Obama becomes president of the United States, how will he deal with black and white race relations?

Since he has stated that America is too divided, will he put forth an effort to bring blacks and whites closer together in the name of improving race relations? That fits perfectly into one of his main campaign slogans, *Change we can believe in.* That's a change of paramount importance that might just get the ball rolling. Obama is the only presidential candidate capable of that accomplishment. Blacks seem to have little interest in listening to what whites have to say about race relations, and older black spokespeople are treating race as though we're still in the 1960s. So now is the time for a younger black individual with the betterment of all America in mind to step up. This is an effort Barack Obama could undertake even if he's not elected. Let's hear it for the bargainers!

Jackie Wilson, because of his musical crossover success, was a bargainer who played an integral part in opening doors for the many black performers who have followed him—although he still receives little appreciation for those accomplishments.

Dr. Martin Luther King Jr. was a challenger only out of necessity, but clearly had the vision to see that the future of a great America lies in the hands of the bargainer.

Al "the challenger" Sharpton was recently described as a media creation, an accurate description indeed. When a legitimate racial incident occurs, why can't the media turn to someone like Colin Powell, Juan Williams, or Larry Elder? Not that these individuals have all the answers—no one does—but at least they possess the intelligence of a bargainer. Instead, the media continues to fuel the flames of racial unrest.

Isn't it odd to note that two of America's best-known challengers are African-American "Reverends" Al Sharpton and Jesse Jackson?

We both, blacks and whites, have a lot to say about one another, but have you ever stopped to notice how little of it is positive? Each and every one of us is capable of turning that around. We need to ask ourselves, "Where is Love?" That, by the way, is the title of a great Jackie Wilson song;

it's the first cut on his last album, *Nobody But You*, and is now the official theme song of this book. Another bit of encouragement from Jackie comes in a duet with Linda Hopkins in their 1963 hit "Shake A Hand," when he's singing the lyrics, "...Don't forget to pray, and shake a little hand each and every day of your life."

We owe it to ourselves to stop racial generalization, something we are all guilty of. To determine if our grievances are legitimate, it's only fair to be specific about what they are and what individual or individuals are believed to be responsible. The government, the justice system, and every ethnicity on the face of the earth are made up of individuals, so logic falls by the wayside, and any sense of fairness gets eliminated when we generalize too much about who and what we are dissatisfied with.

My own personal efforts of reaching out to be fair and kind to individuals of the African-American race seem to be subconsciously affected by my sense of their deep-seated racial generalization of the white population, past and present. Even beyond this difficulty, in my heart, it has always been about the individual.

Every story needs a beginning, middle, and an end. This story has the beginning and the middle, but the end remains out of reach and will continue to be so until the better part of 300 million or so Americans realize that allowing racial divisions to come among us is a detriment to the "unity" of the United States of America.

United, we stand to make the most of what our society offers. Divided, shatters the dream of Dr. Martin Luther King Jr. And mine as well.

Select Bibliography

Books

Carter, Doug Saint. <u>The Black Elvis – Jackie Wilson</u>. Jacksonville Fl.: Heyday Publishing, Inc., 1998
.

Steele, Shelby. <u>A Bound Man: Why we are excited about Obama and why he can't win</u>. New York, NY: Free Press, 2007.

Williams, Juan. <u>Enough</u>. New York, NY: Three Rivers Press, 2006.

Articles and News Accounts

"Alabama apologizes for its participation in slavery," <u>The Florida Times-Union</u> (June 1, 2007).

"Brown: Haiti policy 'racist'," The Florida Times-Union (February 26, 2004).

Brumley, Jeff. "Violence a key issue for new faith office leader," The Florida Times-Union (January 31, 2007).

Burns, Regina. "Civil rights sites are popular school tool," The Florida Times-Union (May 29, 2007).

Grant, Rick. "Doug Saint Carter; Presented lecture on Jackie Wilson at FCCJ" Entertaining U (February 13, 2003).

Henninger, Daniel. "Obama and Race," The Wall Street Journal (February 21, 2008).

"The hurricanes and slave ghosts," Florida Star (September 25, 2004).

Horowitz, David. "Deafening Silence," Jewish World Review (March 20, 2000).

Horowitz, David. "Racial Shakedown," Jewish World Review (February 22, 2000).

"Martin Luther King III and Rev. Al Sharpton to lead march on Washington," Jet (July 10, 2000).

Patton, Charlie. "Whites and blacks alike see racism on the rise," The Florida Times-Union (December 15, 2006).

Parker, Kathleen. "Hostile language by students justifies lawsuit from teacher," The Florida Times-Union (May 18, 2007).

SELECT BIBLIOGRAPHY

McWhorter, John. "Focus: White do-gooders did for black America," The Sunday Times (September 11, 2005).

Runk, David. "Obama wins NAACP's favor at convention forum," The Florida Times-Union (July 13, 2007).

Treen, Dana. "Life in the murder zone," The Florida Times-Union (April 4, 2004).

Trinidad, Alison. "Jacksonville no. 10 as a top city for blacks," The Florida Times-Union (April 18, 2007).

Wheeler, Tracy. "Time against race," The Florida Times-Union (October 30, 2006).

Whitlock, Jason. "Imus isn't the real bad guy," The Kansas City Star (April 11, 2007).

Simerman, John; Ott, Dwight; Mellnik, Ted. "Katrina's ultimate victims: Seniors," The Florida Times-Union (December 30, 2005).

Letters to the Editor/Editorials

Goldberg, Jonah. "Diversity means discrimination against many Asian-Americans," The Florida Times-Union (November 24, 2006).

Hinman, Dan. "Black inmates; The problem is a culture issue," The Florida Times-Union (April 27, 2006).

Murray, Rhonda Strange. "King would be appalled," The Florida Times-Union (January 26, 2006).

Reinsch, Kenneth. "Columnist should face reality," The Florida Times-Union (January 29, 2007).

Sowell, Thomas. "Duke rape allegations are example of justice denied," The Florida Times-Union (May 18, 2006).

Stumin, Constance. "End political correctness," T-You: JCCI Reducing Violence Study. The Florida Times-Union (June 21, 2006).

Online Articles

De Moraes, Lisa. "Kanye West's torrent of criticism, live on NBC," Washingtonpost.com (September 3, 2005).

Elder, Larry. "Congresswoman Cynthia 'Zsa-Zsa' McKinney's greatest hits," Townhall.com (April 13, 2006).

Elder Larry. "'Crash,' the movie vs. race relations, the reality," Townhall.com (March 16, 2006).

"First lady: Charges that racism slowed aid 'disgusting'," CNN.com (September 8, 2005). Full URL: http://www.cnn.com/2005/POLITICS/09/08/katrina.laurabush

"Jesse Jackson urges boycott of 'Seinfeld' DVD box set in wake of 'Kramer's' racist rant," Associated Press (on foxnews.com) (November 28, 2006).

"Jury finds Bevel guilty of double murder," News4Jax.com (August 26, 2005).

SELECT BIBLIOGRAPHY

Kouri, Jim. "Duke rape case premise based on myth," The National Ledger (December 29, 2006).

Lartigue, Casey & Morgan, Eliot. "Talk radio can't handle the truth," washingtonpost.com (August 2, 2007).

"Rapper Kanye West denounces Bush response, American media at hurricane relief telethon," Wikinews.org (September 3, 2005).

Simons, Dana Hawkins. "Getting DNA to bear witness," USNews.com (June 23, 2003).

Steinby, Stephen. "Race Relations: The problem with the wrong name," Wpunj.edu (2001).

Whitlock, Jason. "Vick deserves shot at redemption," Foxsports.com (August 26, 2007).

Interviews

Conrad, Jarik. Personal interview. Chief Administrative Officer of the Jacksonville Regional Chamber of Commerce and the executive director of Blueprint for Prosperity. (May 2007).

Garner, Dwight. "Al Sharpton's second act," Salon.com (April 18. 1996).

Rev. Rudolf Porter. Personal Interview. Mayor's office of Faith and Community Based Partnerships for the city of Jacksonville (February 28, 2007).

Rumlin, Isaiah. (by telephone) Local chapter of the NAACP. (June 2007).

"The O.J. Verdict; Michael Eric Dyson Interview," <u>Frontline, PBS.org</u> (October 4, 2005).

Index

INDEX

INDEX

www.ingramcontent.com/pod-product-compliance
Lightning Source LLC
Chambersburg PA
CBHW020610270326
41927CB00005B/261